HUGH POLAND ■ Foreword by Scott Phillips

P9-CDF-095

the Master Carpenter

DEVOTIONS FOR WOODWORKERS

JUDSON PRESS
PUBLISHERS SINCE 1824

VALLEY FORGE, PA

For Hugh Sr. and Claude,
who allowed me to apprentice

The Master Carpenter: Devotions for Woodworkers
© 2008 by Judson Press, Valley Forge, PA 19482-0851
All rights reserved.

Judson Press and the author have made every effort to trace the ownership of all quotes. In the event of a question arising from the use of a quote, we regret any error made and will be pleased to make the necessary correction in future printings and editions of this book.

Bible quotations in this volume are from HOLY BIBLE: *New International Version*, copyright © 1973, 1978, 1984. Used by permission of Zondervan Bible Publishers.

Library of Congress Cataloging-in-Publication Data
Poland, Hugh. / The Master Carpenter : devotions for woodworkers / Hugh Poland. — 1st ed. p. cm.
Includes index. / ISBN 978-0-8170-1529-9 (pbk. : alk. paper) 1. Woodworkers—Religious life. 2. Woodworking—Religious aspects—Christianity. I. Title.
BV4596.W66P65 2008
242'.68—dc22   2008005901

Printed on recycled paper in the U.S.A. / First Edition, 2008.

CONTENTS

FOREWORD

Once long ago, an earth-moving event changed humanity forever. A humble Jewish carpenter walked up on a mountain and told stories to thousands about how God wants us to live and pray. Just think how inspirational it would have been if we could have heard him speak on that fateful day.

In a real way, *The Master Carpenter* captures that teaching moment by putting imagination into words that Christ embodied in his ministry on earth. Short of the second coming, our daily walk in this world needs inspiration. You'll find such inspiration here.

Hugh Poland is the master of parable. His words are brilliant, connected, and timely. His stories captivate the mind and inspire sleeping questions about Jesus and how he can grace our lives each and every day.

This book will draw in everyone with a spark of faith in their spirit and an ounce of sawdust in their past.

Every library and woodshop should have this book! Keep *The Master Carpenter* close at hand for daily reflection and inspiration as you seek to apprentice yourself to Jesus.

—Scott Phillips
Woodworker of *The American Woodshop* on PBS

PREFACE

In the opening scenes of the movie *The Passion of the Christ,* Jesus is hard at work crafting a chair. I vividly remember the excitement he showed as he explained to his mother that they could sit in chairs at the table rather than recline. While this is purely conjecture on the screenwriter's part, it nonetheless reminds us right away that Jesus—the son of our Creator—was being a creator himself. And he's still a carpenter today—a Master Carpenter—and I consider myself to be one of the many tools in his tool-box. As a disciple of Christ Jesus, I give my life to him to use for whatever he wants to build on this earth.

As the tools editor for the world's largest woodworking magazine, I can instantly relate. Hugh Poland does an exceptional job of connecting faith and life in Christ to every aspect of woodworking. From planning out your next project, to choosing, using, and maintaining your tools; from selecting the best material for the job, to machining it and joining it together, and finally bringing it to a finish, Hugh walks us through each phase of our "project development."

Just as when we work with wood, Hugh shows that in working out our faith we need to experience the bad times (does anyone *really* like sanding?) as well as the good times (like when a dovetail joint slips together perfectly) in life to condition us fully according to God's master plan. God takes each of us from the rough lumber of our sinful lives apart from him, and then shapes and molds us with his Holy Word, joins us to other believers for strength and support, and then refines us with joys, sorrows, love, peace, happiness, and trials until we are as he envisioned us.

Woodworkers will appreciate Hugh's creative and thought-provoking approach in providing daily lessons that lead us, as apprentices to the ultimate master, as we strive to become more like the one and only Savior, Jesus.

—Bob Hunter
Tools & Techniques Editor
WOOD magazine

ACKNOWLEDGMENTS

I WOULD LIKE TO THANK those at Judson Press who have greatly encouraged me throughout this process. Rebecca Irwin-Diehl and Kim Shimer have not only been a tremendous help, they have been wonderful friends as well. The staff and worship teams at my church, Woodridge Baptist Church of Kingwood, have blessed me with much love and support. And of course, my wife, Karen, and daughters, Kayse, Jayme, and Ally, have created a place of love and laughter where anything can happen—and often does. We may not live in a castle, but let's continue to build our dream home together.

INTRODUCTION

A survey of the garage on this chilly December morning points out my deficiencies and raises the notion that my name and "Master Carpenter" don't belong on the same piece of paper.

The workbench is crowded with extra screws that don't fit any project, but I'm too cheap to throw them out. An extra lightbulb sits in its box on top of a radio, and a garden hose reel lies haphazardly on a table, waiting to roll off and fall on my foot when I least expect it. A woodworking magazine is opened to the plans for a cherry sleigh bed, mocking my best intentions and my lack of abilities. Bicycle handlebars catch my shirt in almost any direction I turn.

But what keeps me coming back to the bench and its surrounding tools are the stacks of wood on the other side of the garage. There's enough walnut for a nice tabletop, if I get my courage up to make the first cut into it. There's some cedar for those outdoor planters I've been promising my wife. Cherry sits waiting, harvested from a tree my mother used to climb as a small girl. Small pieces of oak and ash hover around the lathe, waiting to be chosen for a special task. Clear cypress is bountiful, and even some pieces of mesquite and purpleheart are in supply. Long pine boards from a sinker log, harvested from the Neches River where my grandfather worked for a logging company almost 100 years ago, definitely qualify as "old growth." (This also explains why we park our cars in the driveway!)

Does the smell of sawdust seduce you? Do you enjoy going to the "tool and drool" store? Is your TV permanently switched to the Home and Garden Channel? Is each piece of lumber in your shop like that one good shot in a round of golf that keeps a duffer coming back for more? If you're just one accurate measure, one smooth cut, one patient sanding away from a satisfying project, then you have a lot more in common with the Master Carpenter than you think.

One of the reasons many of us get into woodworking is so that we might build something that will say to the rest of the world, "I was here"; to construct something that will outlive us and be treasured by another generation. The wise King Solomon once said of God, "He has set eternity in the hearts of men" (Ecclesiastes 3:11). Do you see this truth in your own life?

Do you burn to create something that outlives you, something that will have an impact on your descendants, something that points them toward ultimate truth? Don't we long for our children to grow up and accomplish greater things than we ever dreamed possible?

Well, with human beings these things are impossible, but with God all things are possible. And that's what this book is about.

There are tons of how-to books out there. This book isn't one of them. If you're like me, you don't need another book of woodworking plans or instructional manuals. You already know what to do with your tools.

Instead, think of this book as a collection of life plans you can read in the next couple months. You do not need another book telling you right from wrong—you already know that—but you may need a Master Carpenter to come into the shop of your heart and demonstrate a few useful life techniques, give you a little correction here and there, and inspire you to do what you already know to do.

You may want to reach for this book as you grab your first cup of coffee in the morning. Take a few minutes before the wood chips start to fly. Pull up a stool next to your workbench, and read one of the short chapters. You just might find yourself learning at the feet of the Master Carpenter himself. You might also see that your name *does* belong next to his.

And if it helps you fall in love with Jesus a little bit more, it will all be worthwhile, won't it?

Plans

[David] gave [Solomon] the plans of all that the Spirit had put in his mind for the courts of the temple of the LORD and all the surrounding rooms, for the treasuries of the temple of God and for the treasuries for the dedicated things.

—1 Chronicles 28:12

It pays to plan ahead. It wasn't raining when Noah built the ark.

—Unknown

May he give you the desire of your heart and make all your plans succeed.

—Psalm 20:4

When evil men plot, good men must plan. When evil men burn and bomb, good men must build and bind. When evil men shout ugly words of hatred, good men must commit themselves to the glories of love.[1]

—Martin Luther King Jr.

"For I know the plans I have for you," declares the LORD, "plans to prosper you and not to harm you, plans to give you hope and a future. Then you will call upon me and come and pray to me, and I will listen to you. You will seek me and find me when you seek me with all your heart."

—Jeremiah 29:11-13

TEKTON

Jesus left there and went to his hometown, accompanied by his disciples. When the Sabbath came, he began to teach in the synagogue, and many who heard him were amazed.

"Where did this man get these things?" they asked. "What's this wisdom that has been given him, that he even does miracles! Isn't this the carpenter? Isn't this Mary's son and the brother of James, Joseph, Judas and Simon? Aren't his sisters here with us?" And they took offense at him.

Jesus said to them, "Only in his hometown, among his relatives and in his own house is a prophet without honor." He could not do any miracles there, except lay his hands on a few sick people and heal them. And he was amazed at their lack of faith.

—Mark 6:1-6

Carpentry is one of the world's oldest and most honorable professions. Since the beginning of time there have been men and women who have dedicated themselves to learn skills that would provide shelter, furnishings, utensils, and even recreational items for people. And isn't that just like Jesus, to find yet one more way to provide for us while he was here on earth? Can you imagine owning a chair or bed that was handcrafted for you by the son of Joseph, Jesus the carpenter?

I find it ironic, and I'm not the first to say so, that the very cedar he shaved with a plane was from a tree he spoke into existence at the beginning of time. As he built a spruce tabletop, he remembered saying "Let the land produce vegetation" when he created its mother tree. And if he cut timber to build a house for someone, it had to remind him that he would someday go to prepare another place for his followers to live.

And yet his greatest masterpiece of carpentry came from two rough-hewn timbers that looked for all the world like objects of scorn, but have become for us the ultimate masterpiece of carpentry. No exquisitely garnished cabinetry, no impressively shaped furniture, no palace of royalty will ever come close to the artisan craftsmanship that is the cross.

He could have come as a king and impressed us with his riches.

He could have come as a military leader and demanded our loyalty.

Instead, he came as a blue-collar worker, a man with sawdust in his pores and splinters in his hands. A man who wasn't afraid of manual labor and a little elbow grease. Good thing—the human race needed someone to labor over them.

He came as one who knew that the human heart needed a major makeover. And unlike the popular TV shows of our day when people leave and their houses are remodeled in a weekend, Jesus knew that the task of reshaping and reforming and reclaiming the human heart would take much longer and cost much more than a coat of paint, a recovered sofa, and a hastily constructed set of MDF shelves.

He came as a carpenter of love to undertake the most ambitious building project of any leader in the history of the universe. He came to rebuild the human heart, whose walls and chambers and windows had been ravaged by the effects of sin.

Through the years, many have wondered about the vocation of Jesus. The Greek word *tekton* is translated "carpenter," but it really refers to one who works in stone, iron, and copper, as well as in wood. So he could have been skilled in a variety of trades.

But others who lived in the era immediately following Jesus also taught that he was a carpenter. Justin Martyr, a famous defender of the faith in the second century, wrote, "And when Jesus came to the Jordan, He was considered to be the son of Joseph the carpenter; and He appeared without comeliness, as the Scriptures declared; and He was deemed a carpenter (for He was in the habit of working as a carpenter when among men, making ploughs and yokes; by which He taught the symbols of righteousness and an active life)."[1]

Other early church leaders also connected Jesus with the vocation of carpentry. Joseph followed Jewish tradition by passing his skills on to his adopted son. One rabbinical saying was "whoever does not teach his son a trade, it is as if he brought him up to be a robber." Jesus was no robber, unless one considers that he had come into the world to steal our hearts back from the enemy and restore us to a former glory. But he was a carpenter, a worker with wood, and we would do well to become his apprentices.

Apprenticeship: *Carpenter of Love, I'm sure there have been times that you have been amazed at my lack of faith. I long to see wondrous signs and miracles, but I haven't the spiritual eyes to see you for who you really are.*

Take me to your workbench today. Pull your tools out and begin the work of reshaping my life. I will submit to the blade that cuts away the strongholds of sin. I will yield to the sandpaper that smoothes my rough edges. I will receive that coat of stain that brings out the beauty in my life. Do a major makeover in me, O Lord, that when others see me I may be a reflection of your excellent craftsmanship.

OH, I GET IT!

As Jesus was walking beside the Sea of Galilee, he saw two brothers, Simon called Peter and his brother Andrew. They were casting a net into the lake, for they were fishermen.

"Come, follow me," Jesus said, "and I will make you fishers of men." At once they left their nets and followed him.

Going on from there, he saw two other brothers, James son of Zebedee and his brother John. They were in a boat with their father Zebedee, preparing their nets. Jesus called them, and immediately they left the boat and their father and followed him.

—Matthew 4:18-22

subscribe to a couple different woodworking magazines, and I always find myself picking up more at the local grocery store. I enjoy dreaming, learning new techniques, seeing pictures of finished work, reading about tools, and looking at plans for my next project. They are all well written by people who genuinely want to pass on their knowledge and expertise. They are, however, no substitute for the real thing: hands-on experience alongside a master carpenter.

I'm the kind of person who needs to see a demonstration. I want to see someone doing it in front of me, talking through the process. For every pro that writes a "how-to" in a magazine, there are thousands of weekend warriors like me who haven't had all the training we need. It's like a singer getting a private lesson from Tony Bennett, or a cook working alongside Emeril Lagasse. I still wish Scott Phillips would show up in my garage wearing a toolbelt and ask, "Can I be of any help?" I need someone who already does it better to show me the way, to let me put my hands on the project, and then gently guide me through the process, all the while encouraging me as I falter and make mistakes.

The word "apprentice" comes from a Latin word that means "to seize or apprehend." But in today's vernacular, when a light bulb goes off in our head, we don't say "Now I seize the truth." Instead we say, "Oh, I get it!" (Younger people distill it down to one word: "Cool.") Typically, an apprentice trains for about four years while learning more than fifty different skills and techniques. There's plenty that can be gained by reading, but a carpenter's apprentice learns while on the job. It's in the doing of the work under the supervision of a carpenter that new skills are developed. Once an apprentice "gets it" and becomes competent in one area of expertise, he moves on to more advanced skills. Eventually, the apprentice takes a test to become a journeyman carpenter.

Isn't it great that we have a savior who allows us to apprentice beside him! He could have simply told the twelve disciples, "Read these particular scriptures and religious writings, then come take a test. If you make the grade, I'll be your friend." Instead, Jesus allowed his disciples to hang out with him in the classroom of everyday life. He simply called them to follow him, and they left everything behind to do so. No doubt they studied the written word of God, but they *walked* with the Living Word of God.

They watched him accept children whom they had turned away, and they learned how to come into the kingdom of God (Matthew 19:14). They saw his devotion to his Father in the early hours of the morning (Mark 1:35) and realized they needed the same passion in their prayer life. They picked up leftovers after the miraculous feeding of the multitude (John 6:13) and held in their hands proof that God provides. They felt the waves pound fear into their hearts as their boat got caught in a storm, and then experienced the warmth of the sun on their faces as their passenger spoke peace to the wind and the waves (Mark 4:41). They saw him forgive his enemies (Luke 23:34), and it empowered them to do the same.

You can't learn to hit a curveball simply by reading an article about Babe Ruth. You'll never work that slice out of your drive off the tee merely by watching Tiger Woods on the Golf Channel. Some woodworkers can learn a great deal by simply reading the project plans, but it isn't the same as having a master carpenter in the shop, one who patiently guides, corrects, and encourages us in our work. We all need someone to enable us to say, "Oh, I get it!" Or, if you want, "Cool!"

Apprenticeship: *Master Carpenter, help me to "get it"—to really understand your work in my life, and learn from you. You have so much to teach me, and I am so slow to learn at times. Thank you for your patience. I pray that when the tests of life come, I'll fall back on the training I have received from you in the time we have spent together. When difficulties arise, may I draw strength from knowing I am your apprentice, and that you have promised you will not abandon the project of my heart, but will continue your good work in me until I am completely finished (Philippians 1:6).*

THE DIT CHANNEL

> Let us consider how we may spur one another on toward love and good deeds. Let us not give up meeting together, as some are in the habit of doing, but let us encourage one another—and all the more as you see the Day approaching.
> —Hebrews 10:24-25

If you're a woman reading this, please pardon me for a moment while I address the guys. It has to do with television and remote controls. I know, I know. Men are accused of not really caring what's on TV. They only want to know what *else* is on TV, and so they (ok, we) channel surf between sports, war movies, and the Do-It-Yourself Channel. Actually, some of the more popular channels on television today are the ones that appeal to "DIY-ers" (Do-It-Yourselfers). Mention the words "honey-do" list, minor home repair, or DIY, and I immediately think of either Norm Abram or Tim Taylor.

Norm, of course, is the *crème de la crème* of woodworkers, having hosted *This Old House* and *New Yankee Workshop* and written about a dozen books on the subject. Clad in his familiar flannel shirt, you get the impression that Norm would make a great next-door neighbor.

"Uh, my garage door is stuck, Norm. Can you fix it?"

"Sure, Hugh, and while we're at it, let's build a new garage, put a woodshop in one corner, a fireplace in the other, and a media center with a fridge along the far wall. That way when you've upset your wife, you'll have someplace to go!"

Funny guy, that Norm. The truth is, many of Norm's projects are out of my grasp. Either I don't have the tools, or I lack the experience to do it like Norm.

But neither do I want to DIY like the fictional character, Tim "The Toolman" Taylor, the handyman/TV show host on the old hit sitcom *Home Improvement*. Tim was forever getting into projects over his head. In fact, usually because he didn't *use* his head he ended up *hurting* his head. Super Glue and horsepower were a near-lethal combination for poor Tim. The character, played so well by comedian Tim Allen, is a funny yet all-too-real reminder of what happens when macho bravado gets in the path of any power tool.

Along the same lines, Christianity is not a DIY weekend project, though many men try to make it just that. How hard can it be, right? There's no need to read the instruction manual, rub shoulders with other guys, gain practical faith experience, or actually produce something in the workshop of my heart, right? Let me just show up for an hour on Sunday, pass the plate, punch the clock, and head home to watch the ball game when it's over. It's as easy as using a remote control, right?

Except, the words "do-it-yourself" don't occur anywhere in the Bible. Instead, we find terms like army, community, together in one accord, clan, fellowship, three, twelve, seventy, tribe, and choirs. Even the bride of Christ is not a person but a group of people, the church. But the only book of Scripture in which you'll find the phrase "Pull yourself up by your bootstraps" is the book of 2 Hallucinations. The Bible doesn't use words like hermit, recluse, loner, detached, isolated, monkish, or solo to describe Christ-followers. In fact, of all the singing in the Book of Revelation, of all the songs of praise, there is not one solo—all the praise music of heaven seems to be sung by a choir!

To be sure, there are times we need to practice the discipline of solitude and be alone for a while to pray, to study the Scriptures, and to work out our salvation in our hearts. But the passage in Hebrews says we should regularly meet together to spur one another on toward good deeds, to encourage one another.

Look at it this way—the toolbox of your soul isn't complete without other guys. Your friends are significant tools in the hands of the Master Craftsman, and without them, his work on you and in you will be incomplete.

Even Jesus, who was totally perfect, needed friends. Sure, he had the crowds. There were 120 special followers who waited for the coming of the Holy Spirit in Acts 2. Luke mentioned seventy-two dedicated workers that were sent out by Jesus. But there were twelve who followed him for three years, and three (Peter, James, and John) who were especially close to him. And of those three men, John seemed to be regarded as the most special. So if Jesus, the totally perfect Son of God, needed other people to help him keep going, how much more do you need friends to help sustain you?

Are you part of a church? Good. Are you part of a small group of guys that meet together regularly and discuss sports, woodworking projects, and what God is doing in your life? Even better. Are you encouraging them and account-able to them? Then you're going to be the best at whatever God has for you.

Channel surf onto the DIY Channel for some great home improvement ideas and inspiring projects. But then tune into the DIT Channel for real liv-ing—that's the "Do It Together" Channel.

Apprenticeship: *Lord, my tendency as a man is to do things my way—to try to impress upon others that I don't need them. But deep down inside, I know I really do. I have this tendency to compete with others, to try and outdo their successes, to show the world that I can make it on my own. Lord, help me to develop transparent friendships with others, and help me be vulnera-ble enough to talk on a deeper level with them about my faith in you.*

WHAT ARE YOU BUILDING?

Then Moses said to the Israelites, "See, the LORD has chosen Bezalel son of Uri, the son of Hur, of the tribe of Judah, and he has filled him with the Spirit of God, with skill, ability and knowledge in all kinds of crafts—to make artistic designs for work in gold, silver and bronze, to cut and set stones, to work in wood and to engage in all kinds of artistic craftsmanship. And he has given both him and Oholiab son of Ahisamach, of the tribe of Dan, the ability to teach others."

—Exodus 35:30-34

If you've ever spent time wandering through one of those popular baby name books, you probably haven't given much consideration to the name Bezalel. It may sound like a brand name for flooring adhesive or a specialty wrench, but his name actually has a powerful meaning. Bezalel can mean "in the shadow of Elohim" or "in the protection of God," which is not a bad place to be, especially when operating power tools. At any rate, it's a name mentioned in scripture, and for that reason alone we should take note of it.

Bezalel was sort of the Bob Vila or Scott Phillips of his day. He not only did excellent work, he taught others how to do it, too. He was specially commissioned to build things for the tabernacle—everything from the tent of meeting and the ark of the covenant (Exodus 37:1) to the tables, the candlesticks, the altar and its vessels, and the priestly garments for Aaron and his sons. Bezalel wasn't churning out your average band saw box or turned-pen gift for craft shows. Instead, he had been hired to construct the very place in Hebrew worship where God would dwell with his people and wipe away their sins. In short, he was commissioned to build the house of God!

Bezalel was also controlled by the Spirit of God, so he carried out the work just like the Lord commanded. This suggests he had an eye for detail, performing the work just the way his master wanted it. He had a heart to obey. In addition, he was able to teach others. A fine craftsman, a dedicated follower of God, and a teacher. Some guys seem to have it all, don't they?

So, how would *you* go about building a house for God?

The story is told of a great man who wanted to build his dream house. After the architect finished the design, the man hired a builder with the simple instructions: "Build the finest house possible. Money is not an object. When you're finished there will be a nice bonus for you."

As the months went by, the house began to take shape. But the builder thought he could increase his profit margin a little more if he compromised in a few areas. He used a lower grade of steel in the foundation and cheaper materials in the roofing of the house. The windows—well, they weren't the nice insulated windows the plans called for. The flooring wasn't really solid-wood flooring; it was just a laminate. The paneling wasn't actual mahogany; it was pine, stained to look like mahogany. The walls received just one coat of a cheaper paint. The fixtures in the bathrooms looked nice, but they weren't designed to last a very long time. All these changes saved the builder a lot of money, which he was able to keep in his own pocket.

When the house was finally finished, the great man threw a party and invited his friends and family, and the builder came. The man made an announcement on the front steps of the house before letting everyone in. He said, "As you know, this house has been built by my friend the builder. I gave him instructions to build the finest house possible. I told him money was no object, and I told him there would be a bonus for him when the project was finished." The builder was licking his chops, anticipating a great monetary reward.

"Here you are," the man said to the builder, and handed him the keys to the house. "All you built is yours. I'm giving you the house you built for me. It now belongs to you."

Ouch! What are you building with? You will one day reap the crowns or the consequences of the life you have built. Your work will be shown for what it is. You and I will someday stand before the One whose eyes are like fire, and the fire will test the quality of our work. You, in a sense, *are* a house for God. He does not reside in a tabernacle of stone or wood today. Instead, the tabernacle of God is with us here on earth. He has chosen to live in the hearts of people. The house you are building for God is *you*.

Apprenticeship: *Master Carpenter, I need a building inspection of my life, and you are the only one qualified for the job. Come and look closely at the foundation of my heart, what I have built my life upon. Crawl up in the attic and see the junk I have hidden away in the dark corners of my mind. The power system has some short circuits in places where I've neglected your Word and prayer. When winds of adversity blow, my windows seem drafty. At times I've given in to flashy fixtures and other ornaments that won't stand the test of time. Let's rebuild the home of my heart together, one room at a time.*

FOLLOW THE DIRECTIONS

This is the account of Noah. Noah was a righteous man, blameless among the people of his time, and he walked with God. Noah had three sons: Shem, Ham and Japheth.

God said to Noah, "I am going to put an end to all people, for the earth is filled with violence because of them. I am surely going to destroy both them and the earth. So make yourself an ark of cypress wood; make rooms in it and coat it with pitch inside and out. This is how you are to build it: The ark is to be 450 feet long, 75 feet wide and 45 feet high. Make a roof for it and finish the ark to within 18 inches of the top. Put a door in the side of the ark and make lower, middle and upper decks. I am going to bring floodwaters on the earth to destroy all life under the heavens, every creature that has the breath of life in it. Everything on earth will perish. But I will establish my covenant with you, and you will enter the ark—you and your sons and your wife and your sons' wives with you. You are to bring into the ark two of all living creatures, male and female, to keep them alive with you. Two of every kind of bird, of every kind of animal and of every kind of creature that moves along the ground will come to you to be kept alive. You are to take every kind of food that is to be eaten and store it away as food for you and for them." Noah did everything just as God commanded him.

—Genesis 6:9-22

OK, admit it. You get that exciting new electric thingydobber home and set it up in your garage. You couldn't live without one, and now this new tool is guaranteed to make your work look like the front cover of your favorite woodworking magazine—and the first thing you throw aside as you're opening the box is the directions.

I'll be the first to admit; I do it too. I'm so overcome with the sheer excitement of tearing into my new electrogizmo that those directions, printed in six different languages, no less, just seem to be in the way. Besides, I already know all that stuff, right?

Until it came time to set up my radial arm saw.

Oh my goodness! So many steps. And the directions stated that each step would have to be precisely accomplished, done in order, or I would have to start all over.

Do you ever read the funny stories in some woodworking and handyman magazines where people write in and tell how they didn't read the directions and ruined a project? The amount they get paid for the inclusion of their little story in the magazine doesn't usually make up for the cost of redoing the project.

My first cuts with the saw were less than successful. The main reason I wanted a radial arm saw was to be able to make perfectly square cuts, over and over again, without thinking about it. My goal was to leave the saw set to make perfect 90-degree cuts. But my first attempts looked like they were about 88 degrees.

Now, 88 degrees isn't bad if you don't mind doors that don't align, cabinets that rock back and forth, and picture frames that almost fit together. Of course, these things *are* important to me, so I kept trying to tweak the machine to make my cuts square.

I went back over the instructions and found a simple carriage bolt that I hadn't tightened. Naturally, I couldn't just tighten the bolt. I had to start from the beginning and go through all the steps again before the blade finally aligned to 90 degrees.

The Bible is the primary way God gives us direction for our lives. So why do we try again and again to live without paying any attention to the instruction book?

One word—pride.

God gave Noah explicit instructions about the construction of the ark, and Noah did everything as God commanded him. God is a God of detail, and he is infinitely concerned with each detail of our lives. He didn't just give Noah a pat on the back and say "Better build a big boat—I know you've never seen one before, Noah, but don't let that bother you—a storm is approaching." Instead, he walked Noah through specific details regarding the composition, the size, and the finish of the ark. God also gave Noah explicit instructions regarding the cargo the ark was to carry.

As you read in Hebrews 11:7, Noah built the ark with a spirit of reverence—a spirit of profound, adoring, and awed respect for God, a spirit unlike any other concern he would show for anyone else. In other words, he followed God's directions to a "T." They may have seemed strange. As an inland resident, Noah most likely had never seen a ship before. Some folks even think he had never seen rain before (based on Genesis 2:5). I'm guessing he probably hadn't even seen all the animals before that showed up on his list to procure and board. (If he had seen and experienced mosquitoes before, I think he would have asked "Lord, are you sure?")

But Noah—evidently a man who possessed carpentry skills and went on to become the world's first shipbuilder—obeyed God at all points in this story. Complete, total obedience.

Sometimes our problem is that we tend to run toward "selective obedience." We tend to compartmentalize our lives. A compartment for church on Sunday morning, a compartment for how we work Monday through Friday, and a compartment for how we relax on the weekend. We try to live a life divided into "God-time" and "all-other-time." We conveniently reread the portions of our Bible that are highlighted, the stories and parables and instructions that we agree with, the ones that make us feel good about ourselves.

Perhaps it's time to read some of the passages that we've been ignoring, those that aren't underlined. For instance, did you know Jesus told more stories about money than he did about heaven and hell? Have you noticed how he often turned away people who said they were ready to follow him? And reread that passage of Paul's where he lists those who won't be in the kingdom of heaven (Ephesians 5:3-5). Sometimes we gloss over these truths, like—like instructions for a new tool. Just remember, selective obedience isn't really obedience at all. It's like a radial arm saw that looks good on the outside but has one loose bolt that will cause the entire tool to fail to perform up to standard.

Pull your Creator's instruction manual out again. It's good to read it with your eyes, but even better to store it up in your heart. That's when real life change begins, as you act upon what you read.

Apprenticeship: *Master Instructor, I am guilty at times of building my life without reverence for you and your Word. I've ignored the details of your owner's manual for my life, choosing what I will read and obey, and what I will not. I admit that the ship of my life will take on water and fail to be seaworthy on the storms of life if I don't follow your instructions. I will never be a tool that fulfills its purposes if I fail to live with reverence and awe before you. Come be my trainer, my tutor in all things. I will be your faithful apprentice.*

PICTURE FRAMES

But we have this treasure in jars of clay to show that this all-surpassing power is from God and not from us. We are hard pressed on every side, but not crushed; perplexed, but not in despair; persecuted, but not abandoned; struck down, but not destroyed. We always carry around in our body the death of Jesus, so that the life of Jesus may also be revealed in our body. For we who are alive are always being given over to death for Jesus' sake, so that his life may be revealed in our mortal body.

—2 Corinthians 4:7-11

When I realized how expensive it was to have even simple pictures matted and framed professionally, I began to build some of my own frames. I also invested in a matte cutter and learned how to give prints a more professional touch. Being a collector of autographed baseball memorabilia, I enjoy decorating my office with pictures of favorite players bordered by their team colors.

Most of the frames I make consist of various pieces of trim molding. Once you get a bead on cutting perfect 45-degree miters, they really aren't that difficult. My frames aren't very ornate. A trip to an art museum will reveal much more elaborate frames that are carved with ornamental motifs and gilded with silver or gold. I just aim for a functional way to display photos.

A good frame should crop its subject in such a way that it complements the artwork, yet it shouldn't draw so much attention to itself that the artwork is forgotten. While there have probably been special art exhibits dedicated to frames, ultimately people go to galleries to see the masterpieces that are inside the frames. The best frame is one that is congruous with the masterpiece it holds against the wall. But the *magnum opus* is what is revealed by the frame—the picture!

It is the hardest lesson in life we ever learn. We are not the masterpiece—we are the frames, designed to carry the Artist's glory. Life is not about us; it's about God. Our job is to frame a portrait of grace every day, to give the world another glimpse of the beauty of Christ. In a similar fashion, the apostle Paul compares us to jars of clay that would have little outward beauty or value but would carry treasure of enormous value.

A frame should correspond to whatever it borders. It should complement and not compete with its subject. Imagine having a beautiful photo of your family on your desk at work, cropped by an ugly frame. Your family would be less than honored.

There is something else that is taken for granted when framing pictures: The glass needs to be clean. And while it's easy to wipe the smudges and fingerprints from the outside, sometimes I have to dismantle a frame and pull out the picture, because I forgot to wipe clean the inside of the glass.

We won't frame God's glory perfectly, but he does want us to be clean frames, regularly allowing him to dust us and wipe off the dirt and oils of sin that stick to us as we are handled by the world. And occasionally, he has to take us apart to clean the inside thoroughly. Sure, hard times come. That pressure and persecution that Paul wrote about is real. But the first five words of that passage of Scripture sum it up: "But we have this treasure."

It's sort of liberating, isn't it? You don't have to *be* the treasure. But you *have* the treasure. Are you trying to be the frame or the picture in the middle of the frame? And what kind of frame are you? Does your life complement the Master Artist and his Masterpiece, Jesus? Or does your frame distract from his beauty? Let him fashion you and clean you and hang you on the wall of his gallery, as another exhibit that holds his glory.

Apprenticeship: *Jesus, you are the true masterpiece of the universe. The majesty and beauty of the Milky Way, the breathtaking grandeur of the Rocky Mountains, and the seemingly infinite variety of creatures upon the earth all pale compared to the splendor of your beauty. Remind me, Precious Jewel, that I am not the hub at the center of life—you are. Make the frame of my life a clean one. How blessed I am that you would come to live inside this structure, this jar of clay! Through all the highs and lows of my life, may I carry you to the world and put you on display for all to see.*

MADE WITH WONDER

For you created my inmost being; you knit me together in my mother's womb. I praise you because I am fearfully and wonderfully made; your works are wonderful, I know that full well. My frame was not hidden from you when I was made in the secret place. When I was woven together in the depths of the earth, your eyes saw my unformed body. All the days ordained for me were written in your book before one of them came to be.

—Psalm 139:13-16

I have to admit, I've never tried to carve anything, unless you count a turkey on Thanksgiving. (I don't count whittling. I call the guys I hang with the "Spit and Whittle Club," but the carving we do is of a personal variety, limited to friendly post-weekend jabs at the other's favorite football team.)

Freehand carving is a whole other realm of woodworking. My hat is off to those who see a figure imprisoned in a slab of basswood or butternut and, like Michelangelo, simply remove the excess wood until the figure they see is released.

Bob Kall once said, "Guido the plumber and Michelangelo obtained their marble from the same quarry, but what each saw in the marble made the difference between a nobleman's sink and a brilliant sculpture."[1] While Michelangelo is not known to have worked with wood, the principle is true for woodworkers today. We each have the opportunity to work with the finest wood available, but the vision we see sealed up in between the grain lines makes all the difference.

When we begin to create something, we fashion it out of something else. It all starts with the wood. It may be a log that isn't even rough cut yet, but we see inside the log to the inner beauty of the grain, the rich color of the heartwood, and we can picture the finished project before it has been planed, sanded, shaped, and stained.

But all of our creating starts with something that already exists and ends up as something else. At best we take what already exists and simply refashion it, reshape it, and recolor it.

Not so with God. When he created the heavens and the earth, he did so *ex nihilo*, that is, out of nothing. While he later created humankind out of the dust of the earth (Genesis 2:7), he first created the dust of the earth "out of nothing," and he stepped back and declared all that he had made to be good.

In today's culture we've borrowed from the term *ex nihilo*, and we are living in a world that preaches nihilism, the idea that our lives have no meaning, purpose, or value. Nihilism teaches that there is no objective truth; no Supreme Being or Creator, so there is no right or wrong to our actions. Nihilists reject authority, morality, and social custom. And of course, nihilism teaches that our lives have no inherent value, that there is nothing special about us. If nihilism is true, we are no different than any other creature in the animal kingdom; we have no special destiny to fulfill, no Sovereign God watching over our every step, longing for relationship with us, and no hope after this life is over.

How sad! Thankfully, Scripture tells us a different story. A loving God put you together with love and care. You were no random chance circumstance. Even before medical technology could register your presence inside the womb, God knew you were there. He superintended your formation and development with a watchful eye.

And God has a plan for you, one that only you can fulfill. Before you breathed your first breath, God knew your beginning, your end, and everything in between. God has packaged inside of you a combination of talents, gifts, and background unlike anyone else in the entire universe, because he loves you. And his greatest desire is that you would spend eternity with him.

Yes, there is a God who is desperately in love with you, and has a wonderful plan for your life. And his purpose is not to create some utilitarian sink out of your life, but to chip away at the sin that imprisons you and release you to display his glory and beauty for the entire world to see.

Apprenticeship: *Too often, Lord, I try to live as something I am not. I live by my own plans, make my own choices, and assume it's my life to live as I please.*

How wrong of me, God! Forgive me for forsaking your plans for my life. Change my heart to see that my life has great potential as I place it under your control. Help me to submit to the blows of the hammer and the cutting edge of the chisel as you release me from the bondage of sin. May I even embrace my trials, assured that your loving plan for my life is greater than any plan I could conceive on my own.

A MATTER OF STYLE

"Sir," the woman said, "I can see that you are a prophet. Our fathers worshiped on this mountain, but you Jews claim that the place where we must worship is in Jerusalem."

Jesus declared, "Believe me, woman, a time is coming when you will worship the Father neither on this mountain nor in Jerusalem. You Samaritans worship what you do not know; we worship what we do know, for salvation is from the Jews. Yet a time is coming and has now come when the true worshipers will worship the Father in spirit and truth, for they are the kind of worshipers the Father seeks. God is spirit, and his worshipers must worship in spirit and in truth."

—John 4:19-24

What's your favorite style of woodworking? Perhaps you really enjoy recreating some of the Shaker masterpieces. Classic in design, utilitarian in function, crafted with precision and just a hint of simple beauty. Or maybe you enjoy working in the mission style, or the practicality of the arts and crafts movement. If contemporary is your flavor, then you're probably good with freehanding curves and thinking outside the box.

So, what's God's favorite style of woodworking?

Kind of a ridiculous question, isn't it? Since God created the wood and created us, it would seem that he wants us to enjoy our creativity, and that when we use our skills in whatever style we choose, we are glorifying God. Because for that instant we are a picture of God the Creator. It would seem rather than a particular style, God would be more interested in the quality of our work. Does our work reflect his excellence? Does it remind others of God's nature?

No, it doesn't make much sense to ask what God's preferred style of woodworking is. One might as well ask what his favorite color is.

The woman at the well raised a question that, to our modern ears, might sound trivial. After all, we already know what Jesus' answer was. But she was a Samaritan, and her people had been separated from and marginalized by the Jews for generations—in part because the Samaritans chose to worship on a mountain, and the Jews worshipped in the temple at Jerusalem. She thought it was a theological question when she raised the issue with Jesus.

"Which one is it, Prophet? Which kind of worship really honors God? The kind that is offered from the mountaintop, or the kind that is offered in Jerusalem?"

"Neither one," replied the Master. "The ones that really worship God will worship in spirit and in truth." The woman at the well wanted a mandate for the *geography* of her worship. Instead, Jesus gave her a mandate for the *substance* of her worship.

To me, this discussion at the well is reminiscent of our modern worship wars. Congregations around the country are struggling with what I'm sure feels like a theological question: What is God's favorite worship style? What music ushers us into God's presence to "worship in spirit and truth"?

These so-called worship wars have torn churches apart. Brothers and sisters in Christ have attacked each other over the issue of how we should worship. Whether you enjoy your worship with a choir in robes and a majestic pipe organ, or leaders who wear jeans with guitars and drums, let's admit it: At times, we have valued our preferred *style* over the *substance* of worship.

Now, the Bible is very serious about the *Who* of worship. The *Who* should always be Jesus, and Jesus alone. Scripture is very specific about our attitude as we worship. David wrote in Psalm 51:17, "a broken and contrite heart, O God, you will not despise." And the seriousness of worship is made clear when we see we must worship in spirit and in truth.

But Scripture doesn't present the *how* of worship as often as we want. In fact, what "hows" there are seem to be very diverse and reflective of God's creative nature. Do you like choirs? So does God (1 Chronicles 15:27). Do you like trumpets? Seems the Lord is warming up to hit some high notes on one (1 Thessalonians 4:16). Do you enjoy drums? Yep, he's all over that too (Psalm 150:5).

So, how do you know when you've really worshipped? First, keep in mind that worship is more than the songs we sing. Worship is about centering our focus and our very selves on the person and goodness of God. Worship is seeing God for who God is—and that sheds new light on who we are. Therefore, when we experience brokenness about our sin, we'll know we have truly worshipped. When we take the eyes of our hearts off our arrogant selves and focus them on Jesus, we will have gone a long way toward recovering the true jewel of worship. And when spirit and truth finally become more important than form and style, we will have revival.

Apprenticeship: *Jesus, I call you Lord today, not merely a prophet. For I want you to exercise your lordship over every area of my life. That includes my corporate worship. Forgive me for trying to mandate a certain style of worship, for trying to force my tastes and views on others. Teach me instead what it really means to worship you in spirit and in truth. Help me move* *beyond form to embrace the substance of you and declare your worth in full view of everyone. And grant me the maturity to see that when a worship style that I don't understand or even appreciate is employed in my church, you are simply moving in someone else's life for that moment. Because I don't want to make worship about me; I want to make worship about you.*

COST ANALYSIS

"Suppose one of you wants to build a tower. Will he not first sit down and estimate the cost to see if he has enough money to complete it? For if he lays the foundation and is not able to finish it, everyone who sees it will ridicule him, saying, 'This fellow began to build and was not able to finish.' . . . In the same way, any of you who does not give up everything he has cannot be my disciple."

—Luke 14:28-30, 33

While I've never served as the general contractor for my own house, I can imagine the pressure of working with subcontractors and keeping the project on schedule. It's no good, for example, to have the drywall guys ready to start mudding walls if the roofers haven't finished. If the cabinetmaker is waiting on the plumber to do the sink install, things can get dicey. Building a house takes a tremendous amount of planning and coordination. And building a commercial property takes even more.

I remember a church in one of the communities where I lived, a church that began with dreams of greatness. After meeting in a school for a long time, they had grown to the point where they needed their own space. They purchased land, developed plans, broke ground, and almost overnight had a foundation in place. Before long steel was going up, and it looked like the church was in for some exciting times. A big sign advertised to the community that the soon-to-be completed church would be a great place to worship.

But after a few weeks it appeared that the work had ground to a halt. All the heavy equipment was taken off the property, and no progress was made beyond the skeleton of steel. Months went by, and the sign stayed out front, assuring the community that the church would start worshipping in the new building very soon. But it never happened.

Years later I heard the truth of the matter. Somehow the church had miscalculated the cost of the building. In an effort to cut corners, they had poured a foundation that was not thick enough to support the weight of the steel. The foundation had cracked in numerous places, and the steel and concrete needed to be removed before the city inspector would allow so much as a pup tent to be erected on the site.

Ultimately the church disbanded, unable to overcome their infighting and the mistrust of the community. The sign that advertised the new building stayed up for years, mocking the intentions of the church leaders. Because they hadn't calculated the cost, their effort to build a church building actually did more harm than good.

Jesus' words really struck home with the general contractors in his crowd that day, but you don't have to be in construction to imagine the ridicule and shame of starting a project and not finishing it. His point to the crowd was simply, "Don't start following me and later decide you aren't willing to give your all to it."

Dietrich Bonhoeffer once said "Grace is free, but it isn't cheap." In his book *The Cost of Discipleship*, Bonhoeffer described cheap grace as the "preaching of forgiveness without requiring repentance, baptism without church discipline, Communion without confession, absolution without personal confession. Cheap grace is grace without discipleship, grace without the cross, grace without Jesus Christ, living and incarnate."[1]

"Costly grace," Bonhoeffer went on to say, calls us to follow Jesus Christ. "It is costly because it costs a man his life, and it is grace because it gives a man the only true life. It is costly because it condemns sin, and grace because it justifies the sinner. Above all, it is *costly* because it cost God the life of his Son: 'ye were bought at a price,' and what has cost God much cannot be cheap for us. Above all, it is *grace* because God did not reckon his Son too dear a price to pay for our life, but delivered him up for us."

Bonhoeffer continued, "Grace is costly because it compels a man to submit to the yoke of Christ and follow him; it is grace because Jesus says: 'My yoke is easy and my burden light.'"[2]

In short, "When Christ calls a man, he bids him to come and die,"[3] wrote Bonhoeffer, echoing the sentiment of Luke 14:33, "In the same way, any of you who does not give up everything he has cannot be my disciple."

Have you run a cost analysis of what it takes to build your life for Jesus? Is your foundation of faith deep enough to support the building of your life? What part of the word "everything" in v. 33 is confusing to you?

Apprenticeship: *Master, I have longed to build for you, and I want my life to be a thing of excellence that brings you honor and glory. And I would gladly die for you, because you gave your life for me.*

But I struggle to live for you, Jesus. Your call demands that I wake up every morning and put to death my selfishness and pride, my ways of controlling others around me. Please forgive me for desiring a cheap grace. As I add up the spreadsheet of your love for me, I realize I have a deficit in the column that calculates my love for you. Since only a burning desire to follow you will ever do, help me to give my life for you today as a living sacrifice (Romans 12:1-2).

Tools

Therefore do not let sin reign in your mortal body so that you obey its evil desires. Do not offer the parts of your body to sin, as instruments of wickedness, but rather offer yourselves to God, as those who have been brought from death to life; and offer the parts of your body to him as instruments of righteousness. For sin shall not be your master, because you are not under law, but under grace.

—Romans 6:12-14

One only needs two tools in life: WD-40 to make things go, and duct tape to make them stop.[1]

—G. Weilacher

In a large house there are articles not only of gold and silver, but also of wood and clay; some are for noble purposes and some for ignoble. If a man cleanses himself from the latter, he will be an instrument for noble purposes, made holy, useful to the Master and prepared to do any good work.

—2 Timothy 2:20-21

A fool with a tool is still a fool.

—Unknown

Have thy tools ready, God will find thee work.[2]

—Charles Kingsley

RIGHT TOOL, RIGHT JOB

For by the grace given me I say to every one of you: Do not think of yourself more highly than you ought, but rather think of yourself with sober judgment, in accordance with the measure of faith God has given you. Just as each of us has one body with many members, and these members do not all have the same function, so in Christ we who are many form one body, and each member belongs to all the others. We have different gifts, according to the grace given us. If a man's gift is prophesying, let him use it in proportion to his faith. If it is serving, let him serve; if it is teaching, let him teach; if it is encouraging, let him encourage; if it is contributing to the needs of others, let him give generously; if it is leadership, let him govern diligently; if it is showing mercy, let him do it cheerfully.

—Romans 12:3-8

Psychologist Abraham Maslow once said, "If the only tool you have is a hammer, you tend to see every problem as a nail."[1] C'mon, admit it. There have been a few times you've asked a tool to do something for which it wasn't designed.

Ever tried to use a dime for a screwdriver?

Ever cut tile with the crosscut blade in your circular saw?

Have you ever gone really crazy and tried to use the battery end of your cordless drill as a hammer? (Please say it ain't so!)

These episodes are a little commonplace. But if you've ever heard of the Darwin Awards, you know that there are those out there who take using the wrong tool for the wrong job to a new level, and it often results in serious trouble.

How about the guy who jacked up his car, only to find he still didn't have room to work underneath it? To solve the problem, he took the battery out of the car, sat the jack on the battery, then jacked up the car higher and worked underneath it. It worked for a short time. Before the battery exploded and the car fell down.

Then there's the Minnesota man who was working with a drill when he suddenly got an itch in his nose. To scratch the itch, he placed the drill bit up his nose and pulled the trigger to the "on" position. After plastic surgery, he sued the drill manufacturer because there wasn't a warning that came with the tool to instruct consumers not to place the drill up their noses.

Or the tragic story about the guy who needed to drill a hole into the exhaust pipe on his motorcycle. Instead of using a drill, he thought he could achieve the same results with a .38 caliber shell discharged from his gun. Unfortunately, bullets ricochet in ways that drill bits don't.

Professional woodworkers probably laugh and scoff at those of us who have attempted crazy efforts in the past, but it's only because they finally got to a place in their craft where they realized that having the right tool for the right job makes all the difference in the world. Not only is having the right tool much easier and more efficient, it is also much safer.

Sometimes in the church we're guilty of using the wrong tool for the wrong job. Like that soloist in the choir whose voice reminds you of fingernails on a chalkboard. Or that greeter at the front door who needs an extra cup of coffee just to move up to "grouch" from "mean and surly." How about that Sunday school teacher who answers questions people aren't asking and whose weekly lesson is a cure for insomnia?

All these are cases of people who genuinely want to serve the Lord, but are misplaced tools in the wrong area of service. Sometimes it seems like a church doesn't have much choice. Think of it: When someone with a true gift of music and singing decides to just lounge in the pew every week rather than attend choir rehearsal, the result is that someone else less gifted has to step up to the

plate. That grouch at the front door might really be best as a parking lot atten-
dant, but no one else was willing to be a greeter, and he was. And that Sunday
school teacher has a real knack for financial matters and could be serving on
the stewardship committee, but the pastor was begging for more teachers one
Sunday morning, and . . . well, you get the picture.

The phrase that challenges most of us from the Scripture reading above is
"each member belongs to all the others." Simply put, I don't have the right
to withhold my gift from the church.

No one gift is more important than another, which means we are all on
level ground together. It's true that some people have gifts that make them
more visible, such as teaching or singing. Others have gifts that keep them
behind the scenes, such as the gift of service. But both are critical to the work
of the church.

You may look at those on stage every Sunday morning and conclude that
you are more like the "big toe" of the body, or even the armpit. But even these
parts of the body, although they aren't very visible, are crucial to the success
of the overall body. Ever try to walk and balance without a big toe? It's pretty difficult, to say the least. And without armpits, your body temperature
would soar during your woodworking workout.

I think of the man who used his lathe to turn the offering plates my church
uses every Sunday. He would not have sought a visible position of authority,

but he humbly served the Lord wholeheartedly with the gifts and talents God had given him. And the church was the richer for it.

My father was a plumber before he went back to college. To this day he still maintains two main toolboxes, one for carpentry tools and one for plumbing tools. Why? He wants to make sure he has the right tool for the right job. As a kid, when he would ask me to get a tool for him, I often had to ask, "Which toolbox is it in?" No sense in using a plumbing wrench to tighten a bolt on a table leg. No reason to cut a two-by-four with a hacksaw. And he would have groused if I tried to use his crosscut saw to cut copper tubing.

You *are* a tool in God's hands in your local church. Are you the right tool in the right toolbox, ready to be used for the right task?

Apprenticeship: *Great Gift-Giver, I thank you for the fantastic gift of grace that is mine for all eternity. I long to be used by you, but sometimes I wonder if I'm in the right place. I know you have equipped me for your purposes—help me accomplish those purposes as I seek to serve you. May all my gifts and talents be used to shine a spotlight on you, and not upon myself. Establish the work of my hands, Master Carpenter (Psalm 90:17), and help me to do those "even greater things" you told your disciples about (John 14:12).*

THE TOOL YOU CAN'T LIVE WITHOUT

I was there when he set the heavens in place, when he marked out the horizon on the face of the deep, when he established the clouds above and fixed securely the fountains of the deep, when he gave the sea its boundary so the waters would not overstep his command, and when he marked out the foundations of the earth. Then I was the craftsman at his side. I was filled with delight day after day, rejoicing always in his presence, rejoicing in his whole world and delighting in mankind.

Now then, my sons, listen to me; blessed are those who keep my ways. Listen to my instruction and be wise; do not ignore it. Blessed is the man who listens to me, watching daily at my doors, waiting at my doorway. For whoever finds me finds life and receives favor from the Lord. But whoever fails to find me harms himself; all who hate me love death.

—Proverbs 8:27-36

What is the best tool in your garage, the one you can't live without? Some might say their table saw, others the band saw. Someone else hails the biscuit joiner as the tool that has revolutionized her projects, while another would fight you if you tried to take away his battery-operated drill.

So what's the best tool for an apprentice of the Master Carpenter?

It's wisdom.

When God created the heavens and the earth, wisdom was the tool on his belt that he employed the most. When God stretched out the sea, hung the planets and stars in place, and wadded up a stack of mud and called it a mountain, he reached for the wisdom tool. When God formed the wings of an eagle, the legs of a cheetah, and the fins of the killer whale, wisdom was always laying handily on his workbench. And when the Lord breathed life into Adam and Eve, knowing what it would cost him to restore the relationship with humankind once they sinned, wisdom helped him put the finishing touches on creation.

Think of it: The earth hurtles through space at just the right speed, tilt, and rotation, keeping just the right distance from the sun. If even one of these factors were off by just a little bit, life as we know it would cease to exist on earth.

The oceans are just the right depth to balance our atmosphere. If they were much deeper, too much carbon dioxide in our atmosphere would dissolve, affecting life around the planet. (In fact, the rising level of CO_2 in the air is one of the major concerns connected to global warming!)

Consider the heart of the giraffe. One of the strongest in the animal kingdom, it is able to pump blood ten feet up the long neck to the giraffe's brain. Yet what keeps a giraffe from "blowing its mind" when it bends over for a drink of water? A series of valves controls the blood flow at just the right pressure to the brain, and keeps the animal from passing out when it raises its head back up.

That's wisdom incarnate. *Hakam* is the Hebrew word for wisdom. It carries the idea of "living skillfully," or operating one's life with a certain degree of spiritual and practical proficiency. Wisdom, then, is different from knowledge. It's pretty easy to obtain *facts* about the Judeo-Christian God these days, with access to Christian bookstores in your community or on the Internet. Such knowledge of God should not remain merely a set of facts we memorize, like we did when we studied for a test in school. The point at which our knowledge of God intersects with the way we live is the point when we can be said to possess wisdom. Wisdom is knowledge of God that leads to right living.

Just as God kept wisdom as a tool at his side at creation, God wants us to employ wisdom as we daily build our lives. It's that "got-to-have" tool that you'll reach for every day. It will become well-worn with time, yet it will never dull. In fact, it grows stronger the more you use it. There will be a need every day of your life, and you'll be able to pull your wisdom out and apply it, IF . . .

If you've bothered to obtain it. See, the wisdom that comes from heaven doesn't just show up in your heart when you turn eighteen. Or twenty one. Or thirty five. Or fifty five. You don't get it by navel-gazing or meditating on a mountaintop in the Himalayas. So how do you gain this wisdom?

1. ASK FOR IT. James 1:5 says, "If any of you lacks wisdom, he should ask God, who gives generously to all without finding fault, and it will be given to him." Make it part of your daily prayer time, to ask God for the wisdom that comes from the very courts of heaven.

2. LIVE WITH A HEALTHY FEAR OF GOD (Proverbs 1:7). No, this isn't a destructive fear, i.e. "God's gonna get me for what I did wrong!" Instead, this fear is a loving reverence for God that yields to him as the ruler of our life.

3. READ THE BIBLE DAILY, particularly the books of Proverbs and Psalms. Psalm 19:7 says "The law of the Lord is perfect, reviving the soul. The statues of the Lord are trustworthy, making *wise* the simple."

Do you remember your second year in high school or college? The term for a second-year student is sophomore, which is a real oxymoron. The term is probably derived from two different Greek words, *sophos*, which means "wise," and *moros*, which means "stupid." (The latter is where we get our word "moron.")

A sophomore is no longer a lowly freshman. While he or she is not an exalted senior yet, a sophomore can easily lapse into a false sense of security and pride by thinking, "I'm no longer on the bottom like an incoming freshman, so I'm pretty wise in my own eyes." Often a sophomore acts like a smart aleck, a know-it-all, a person who has finally arrived. And in their overinflated sense of competence, they often end up acting the fool. Maybe you've known a couple of sophomores in the woodshop. Those know-it-alls that seem to have more words than wisdom as they operate power tools.

God is no sophomore. The Lord possesses all the wisdom in the universe yet is willing to share it with us as we seek him. Would you say that wisdom is the first tool you reach for when constructing your life? Or are you living as a sophomore, one who possesses some knowledge of God but hasn't let it affect the way they he or she lives?

Apprenticeship: *Lord, I admit that there are sophomoric tendencies in my life. I have an inclination to act proud, as though I have arrived and have no need of you or others.*

But Jesus, you are living wisdom. How I need you to impact the way I live! I'm not satisfied with bits and pieces of information about you, as if I was reading the owner's manual for a tool. Instead, I need you to rev to life my soul within me and affect every relationship, every job, and every dream I have. With the words of the ancient hymn I cry aloud to you,

> *Be Thou my Wisdom, and Thou my true Word;*
> *I ever with Thee and Thou with me, Lord;*
> *Thou my great Father, I Thy true son;*
> *Thou in me dwelling, and I with Thee one.*[1]

FROM PLUMB LINES TO LASER LEVELS

> So this is what the Sovereign LORD says: "See, I lay a stone in Zion, a tested stone, a precious cornerstone for a sure foundation; the one who trusts will never be dismayed. I will make justice the measuring line and righteousness the plumb line; hail will sweep away your refuge, the lie, and water will overflow your hiding place. Your covenant with death will be annulled; your agreement with the grave will not stand. When the overwhelming scourge sweeps by, you will be beaten down by it."
>
> —Isaiah 28:16-18

Few people use a plumb bob (a metal weight that hangs at the end of a plumb line) today to make sure a wall is vertical. A level is much quicker and simpler to use. More recently, laser levels have become all the rage for the weekend warrior and the seasoned construction worker alike. But whatever tool one uses, the end result must be the same. The wall or surface is checked to see if it is "plumb"; that is, will it square up with the next wall or surface?

Whether you are building your dream house or a chicken coop, one rule is sure: You can't end up square and level if you don't start that way. If one wall of the cabinet is not square or plumb, then the rest of the walls of the cabinet will not fit together well. And the bigger the work piece, of course, the more important this is. Being off just a sixteenth of an inch when you begin a cabinet can make the whole project off a quarter of an inch in the end. That means cabinet doors won't line up. It means the piece is not as stable as it might have been. It means it will have to be fixed at some point when the glue in the joints fails. And if the first-floor walls of a multi-story building are not plumb, the building itself becomes rickety, as the walls are unable to carry the load.

When I was in my high school chemistry class, struggling to memorize the periodic table, I always wondered why the symbol for lead was "Pb." I found out later (*after* the test) that it is derived from the Latin word for lead, *plumbum*. Until recently, lead was still the material of choice for pipes in construction (now it's PVC). But we still refer to one who works with the pipes as a "plumber." And the plumb bob at the end of the plumb line string was often made of lead. Thankfully, someone who struggles to get a project square and level isn't called a "plum-bum!"

On a different level, God's standard for "plumb" is righteousness. Not partial righteousness, but total, pure holiness. When it comes to truth, we don't use the word "plumb" much anymore, but the word "on the level" speaks volumes. Are you living a life that is "on the level"? When your life stands next to God's standard, do you match up with it? Or does the wall of your heart lean away from God's benchmark of holy living?

Jesus himself is the plumb-line, the standard of what is true and what is not true. Sometimes people will ask "What is God's opinion about _____?" But an opinion suggests a thought or feeling that is changeable, like a politician responding to the latest poll (or the citizens being polled in response to the latest political statement or maneuver). God doesn't have opinions that he changes from week to week. God doesn't have a "take" on issues, and God has no need to spin details in his favor. God is simply right. Every time.

If your life feels out of balance, off-center, or the ends don't match up—chances are your spirit is out of level. It's not plumb. There's some untruth, some hypocrisy somewhere. It may fool an untrained eye, but you can't hide it from the Master Carpenter.

When a wall is found to be out of plumb, it must be adjusted, and the bigger the wall, the bigger the adjustment. A cabinet might only need a clamp, but forms for a concrete foundation will require a large crowbar. We need to go back to the words of Christ and let them become our standard for living. By submitting our lives to the authority of God's Word, we will make adjustments and begin to match up with the way that Jesus lived.

Apprenticeship: *Precious Cornerstone, I don't have to look at you for very long to realize that my life doesn't match up to yours. Justice and righteousness haven't always been welcome on the construction site of my heart. There are places in my soul that are not on the level. Forgive me for thinking that I could ever hide my sin from you. Use your standard of integrity to straighten the walls of my foundation before my heart sets up in concrete. Make the adjustments that are necessary, that my life might be load-bearing, able to sustain the weight of all you call me to carry.*

TESTED AND PROVEN

His divine power has given us everything we need for life and godliness through our knowledge of him who called us by his own glory and goodness. Through these he has given us his very great and precious promises, so that through them you may participate in the divine nature and escape the corruption in the world caused by evil desires.

—2 Peter 1:3-4

It's fun to go to the local "tool and drool" store. If you're like me, it's hard to walk up and down the aisles of power tools and not covet the latest gadget. If I only had *that* tool, my projects would turn out nicer and be done in a quarter of the time! (Golfers have this same problem: "If I only had *that* club, I'd shave six strokes off my handicap!")

Once I weigh the pros and cons of the purchase (pure bliss in the workshop vs. paying for my children's college education!), I get the tool home and immediately head to the garage to try it. Usually there's some stubborn tape or staples that prevent me from opening the box easily; then I have to dig through a casement of foam that protects it during shipping. Finally, it may need partial assembly, or at least a blade installed. There are always the instructions, but who bothers with those, right? (You *did* read the chapter entitled "Follow the Directions," didn't you?)

Often there's one other thing: A small slip of paper initialed by someone at the factory, stating that this piece of equipment has been quality checked and has passed the inspection. It has been tested and proven, and now it's ready for use.

Major manufacturers test tools in a variety of ways. Often power tools are put through a final test-run under power before leaving the factory. Sometimes they deliberately drop a tool, and if it breaks or malfunctions, all the tools that were created on that production run are also considered failures. Although I take this for granted, it's still reassuring to walk into my shop and throw the switch on the band saw and hear it whir to life. I've tested it and proven it time and again, so I have no reason to believe it will fail me when I need it.

In a conversation with a fellow student during my college years, I noticed that in the margins of his Bible he occasionally wrote the initials "T.P." I asked him what "T.P." meant and he said, "It means tested and proven. I write 'T.P.' beside different promises of God in Scripture, verses that I have seen come true in my own life. I've tested them and proven them to be true, and I won't ever doubt them again."

If it's true, as Peter says, that the promises of God help me escape corruption caused by my evil desires, then I want to know and experience these promises. What promises of God can you write "T.P" beside? Here are some to consider:

- The LORD ... will never leave you nor forsake you. (Deuteronomy 31:8)
- "You will receive power when the Holy Spirit comes on you." (Acts 1:8)
- "Come to me, all you who are weary and burdened, and I will give you rest." (Matthew 11:28)
- Even though I walk through the valley of the shadow of death, I will fear no evil. (Psalm 23:4)
- My God will meet all your needs according to his glorious riches in Christ Jesus. (Philippians 4:19)
- "If you remain in me and my words remain in you, ask whatever you wish, and it will be given you." (John 15:7)
- The one who is in you is greater than the one who is in the world. (1 John 4:4)
- "I am going there to prepare a place for you." (John 14:2)

Spend some time marking some "T.P." verses in your Bible. Thank God that you will never go through a test or a trial and find that his faithfulness is unproven.

Apprenticeship: *Lord, why am I so slow to put your Word to the test? Over and over I find your guarantees throughout Scripture, but I find myself reluctant to believe them or lean on them when times get tough. Help me to get beyond head knowledge of your precious promises and internalize them in the deepest regions of my heart. Make me like a tool that is tested and proven, so that when you want to use me, you can throw the power switch and I'll come to life every time.*

RECHARGING

That evening after sunset the people brought to Jesus all the sick and demon-possessed. The whole town gathered at the door, and Jesus healed many who had various diseases. He also drove out many demons, but he would not let the demons speak because they knew who he was.

Very early in the morning, while it was still dark, Jesus got up, left the house and went off to a solitary place, where he prayed. Simon and his companions went to look for him, and when they found him, they exclaimed: "Everyone is looking for you!"

Jesus replied, "Let us go somewhere else—to the nearby villages—so I can preach there also. That is why I have come." So he traveled throughout Galilee, preaching in their synagogues and driving out demons.

—Mark 1:32-39

One of the most indispensable tools anyone can have is a battery-operated drill. No matter the job you are working on, this tool belongs in your toolbox. If you're like me, you've probably been through several of them. Mine have taken a beating over the years. Imagine having to turn all those screws by hand with a screwdriver or drill out your holes with a ratchet brace. It gives me a great appreciation for the craftsmen who fashioned beautiful furniture centuries ago without the use of power tools. But while I appreciate them, I sure don't want to go back to those days!

The biggest drawback to my drill is that the batteries constantly need to be recharged. I have a small charging station in my shop, and when I'm in the middle of a project, those batteries are being exchanged more than relief pitchers for a last-place baseball team. The charging station is always plugged in, so when I pop a battery into the cradle I know it's wired into power immediately.

I find that my life is a lot like my battery-operated drill. I'd like to think I'm a fairly hard worker, and under the right circumstances, I can accomplish a lot in a single day (though no one is going to accuse me of being indispensable). But the more work I do, the more I need recharge time, time when I'm plugged back into my life's power source. When I'm not consistently recharged, the efficiency of my work slows to a crawl. Eventually, with my spiritual and emotional batteries starved for juice, I will burn out if I don't take some time away from my work and get recharged.

I find consolation in the fact that Jesus needed to do this, too. After all, he wasn't just 100 percent divine, he was also 100 percent human. He got hungry; he experienced the same emotions we experience; and he got tired.

Imagine the scene. Jesus is working hard in the hot sun all day. Then as the sun is setting, does he have a recliner and a TV with remote control underneath a ceiling fan awaiting him? No. Instead, the crowds were waiting outside his door, so many that Mark described them as "the whole town." Who knows how long the time of healing and ministering to people continued? Did the Lord get to bed before midnight? No doubt he was exhausted.

But very early in the morning, while it was still dark, Jesus put the battery of his life in the recharging cradle of his Father's presence. He got away from all who had drained him dry the night before, and just called out to the only one who could sustain him. And he was once again reminded of his Father's purpose for his life. He performed a check on his spirit to make sure he was still aligned with God's ultimate will for his life, the cross.

Maybe in the middle of his exhaustion he questioned God's plan for his life. Perhaps he was even tempted to give up the cross as his goal. He could've stayed there in that hamlet, and the people would have elected him mayor. From there it might have been a stone's throw to greater seats of power. Yet when the disciples came looking for him, flush with the success of an expanding ministry and buoyed by optimism that showed Jesus at the top of the polls, the Lord was not swayed by their message. For he had found rest in his Father and had received marching orders from the throne room of heaven.

"Let's head out, guys," he might have said in our day. "The whole reason I'm here is not to be voted into political power, but so that I can preach the good news of God to others." And with that, the re-energized Jesus dismissed all notions of disobeying his Father's will.

This same Jesus later said "Come to me, all you who are weary and burdened, and I will give you rest" (Matthew 11:28).

When you're in the middle of a stressful day and you feel like everyone needs you, take some time to close the door and get alone with your heavenly Father. After all, a cordless drill with a dead battery is useless in the hands of even the most talented master carpenter.

Apprenticeship: *Lord, I get tired so very easily. It's not just the length of my physical labor each week; it's the inner fatigue I feel when people seem to have a plan for my life, and they need me to conform to their desires. I ask that you would give my body, soul, and spirit the rest they so desperately need. I'm running on empty, Lord, and I need you to recharge me physically, emotionally, and spiritually before I go back out into my work world. Remind me, that you're the only one I really need to live for, and that ultimately, I must follow your plans for my life—plans made in perfect love and perfect wisdom.*

FLOATING A LOANER

The company of the prophets said to Elisha, "Look, the place where we meet with you is too small for us. Let us go to the Jordan, where each of us can get a pole; and let us build a place there for us to live." And he said, "Go."

Then one of them said, "Won't you please come with your servants?" "I will," Elisha replied. And he went with them.

They went to the Jordan and began to cut down trees. As one of them was cutting down a tree, the iron axhead fell into the water. "Oh, my lord," he cried out, "it was borrowed!"

The man of God asked, "Where did it fall?" When he showed him the place, Elisha cut a stick and threw it there, and made the iron float. "Lift it out," he said. Then the man reached out his hand and took it.

—2 Kings 6:1-7

I once had the opportunity to spend a week on a mission trip in Meridah, Mexico, where I was part of a team that built a seminary. Meridah is on the Yucatan Peninsula, close to the equator, so it was very hot and humid on the jobsite.

The construction methods and standards were a little different there. There was no wood framing. Everything was made of concrete. Our job was to build a cinder-block foundation into some extremely rocky ground. Without powerful earth-moving equipment, it was difficult to dig deep enough for the foundation, and I was more than a little concerned about this, especially with the heat approaching 100 degrees. But the missionary indicated to me that it wouldn't be a problem, that he had hired a crew to help us.

"In fact, here comes the crew right now," he said, and I turned around to see a little old man riding a bicycle with a basket mounted on the handlebars. It looked a little funny, as if he was riding a girl's bike and she had her doll collection stashed in a box in the basket.

"He's your crew?" I asked, chuckling. "How's he going to help? What's in the basket?"

"Dynamite," replied the missionary.

At that I stopped laughing and backed up. Way back.

During the time of Elisha, the local seminary needed to be expanded, and the students were eager to make the project happen. As they were chopping down trees and preparing the timber for construction, one took a swing with his axe, only to see the iron axe head fly off the handle and land in the Jordan River.

Now, the Jordan is not to be confused with crystal-clear water found off the beaches of Jamaica. It's muddy, and it's difficult to see your feet if you're standing in more than a couple inches of water. The problem was compounded when the young seminary student explained that the axe wasn't really his, but had been lent to him.

Elisha, who didn't waste words in this story, asked a simple question. "Where did it fall?" Sometimes all it takes to get our lives back on track is a simple question. The seminary student took Elisha back to the place he had first lost the axe head, and God performed a miracle through Elisha. The prophet dropped a stick into the water, the axe head floated, and Elisha told the young man to lift it out.

An axe is a large, heavy, scary-sharp piece of metal that is attached to a wooden handle by the tiniest of metal wedges keeping the head firmly in place. But as the wood of the handle expands and contracts with moisture and constant pounding, the wedge can work loose. And when an axe head flies off the handle, it doesn't discriminate what—or who—it hits. Unfortunately, the erosion of the axe handle doesn't happen overnight. In fact, the erosion is happening even before the user of the axe can tell that the head is working loose.

An axe handle without an axe head is pretty useless when it comes to getting the timber cut down. You can get real busy looking with a handle; you can flail away at a tree; you can make a lot of noise and get real sweaty; but you won't cut down any trees!

It's the business end of the blade that gets the job done, not the handle. A lot of Christians are like that handle—they can be real busy in a church, create a lot of perspiration and noise, but not get the real work of building the kingdom done.

The axe head represents the power to get the work done. The Greek word for power is *dunamis*—and that's where we get our word for dynamite. For Christ-followers today, the Holy Spirit is our power to accomplish small and great things for God. The Spirit's power doesn't come to us packed in a basket on a bicycle, but Jesus himself promised that the power would be ours: "But you will receive power when the Holy Spirit comes on you; and you will be my witnesses" (Acts 1:8).

But like the axe head, like everything we have in this life, the power of the Spirit is borrowed—we don't own it. And the erosion of the Holy Spirit's power from the life of a believer is a slow thing. It's not as if we lose the presence of the Holy Spirit in our lives. But we can certainly quench the Spirit's power. And what do we do when this happens?

We need to be restored. We need the Holy Spirit's power in order to once again live a life of obedience. Go back and figure out when you were first aware of a loss of spiritual power. Perhaps you began to go through a dry time. Or you noticed a gradual shift away from the authority of God's Word in your life. Go back to the place you lost the power. Then ask God for a miracle. He will show you that he's more than capable of floating a Loaner.

Apprenticeship: *Great Three in One, forgive me for presuming that the power of the Holy Spirit is mine apart from being rightly connected to you. I confess that at times I have quenched the power of the Holy Spirit in my life. On many occasions I have shut off the flow of the* dunamis, *the dynamite, the power of the one who came to fill me with power. I need the restoration of the axe head to my handle. Come and bring your* dunamis *to bear in my life. Once restored, may I then be about the business of building, not tearing down, the kingdom of God.*

HITTING THE NAIL ON THE HEAD

When we put bits into the mouths of horses to make them obey us, we can turn the whole animal. Or take ships as an example. Although they are so large and are driven by strong winds, they are steered by a very small rudder wherever the pilot wants to go. Likewise the tongue is a small part of the body, but it makes great boasts. Consider what a great forest is set on fire by a small spark. The tongue also is a fire, a world of evil among the parts of the body. It corrupts the whole person, sets the whole course of his life on fire, and is itself set on fire by hell.

All kinds of animals, birds, reptiles and creatures of the sea are being tamed and have been tamed by man, but no man can tame the tongue. It is a restless evil, full of deadly poison.

With the tongue we praise our Lord and Father, and with it we curse men, who have been made in God's likeness. Out of the same mouth come praise and cursing. My brothers, this should not be. Can both fresh water and salt water flow from the same spring? My brothers, can a fig tree bear olives, or a grapevine bear figs? Neither can a salt spring produce fresh water.

—James 3:3-12

Some consider it a stress release to work with wood. I find it so, but I also consider it unwise to do much in the workshop if I'm feeling frustrated or angry. This is especially true when operating power tools, but even hand tools can take only so much abuse if they are in the hands of someone who is out of control with anger.

Anyone who has ever swung a hammer is familiar with this scenario: You're holding a nail, determined to pound it into a piece of wood. And your brain begins to make calculations at Pentium processor speed—the size of the head on the nail, size of the hammer head, velocity of your forearm, density of the wood, length of the nail, wind speed, amount of arthritis in your wrist—wait, it's a nail, not a tee shot at the U.S. Open! Just hit the nail on the head, right?

So you swing away, and that first blow finds a nail. Unfortunately, it's the thumbnail attached to your body, not the sixteen-penny variety. And from somewhere in the deep cavern of your soul, a word is formed. As your brain is calculating the compression of your thumb, a sharp stinging sensation rushes through your nervous system and back to your thumb, and it is somehow like a rope that quickly yanks the word all the way to your lips like a water skier is yanked off the pier by a boat in one of those funny video shows. The word, which you first heard as a kid, passes over your vibrating vocal cords, past your tongue and teeth, and is out for public consumption for anybody within fifty yards.

It's not a nice word.

You're probably more spiritual than I am, and this has never happened to you, right? But it sure has happened to me, and more than once.

No "devil made me do it." No blaming the way your parents raised you. No "If there's no one around when I did it, it doesn't really count" reasoning.

The tongue is a mirror to the heart. It only reflects what we hold up in front of it. You could say that the tongue is like a computer. A computer can only do what it is programmed to do. (Even though I often accuse my computer of having an artificial intelligence that wants to leave me high and dry when I'm facing a deadline, I know ultimately a computer can't act on its own.)

The tongue can only do what it has been programmed to do. It just shows off my programmed ego, insecurity, selfishness, lack of self-control, and my desire to be God. Nothing comes from the tongue that wasn't in the heart first. Our tongue merely reflects whatever is present in our heart.

In Matthew 12:34-35, Jesus confronted the religious leaders of his day and said "You brood of vipers, how can you who are evil say anything good? For out of the overflow of the heart the mouth speaks. The good man brings good things out of the good stored up in him, and the evil man brings evil things out of the evil stored up in him." Just another reminder that the tongue is merely a symptom of a bigger problem.

At first glance, James doesn't seem to give us much hope that our tongue can be tamed. But then he talks about the fig tree and gives us a clue on how we might change.

I'm no botanist, but in lay terms, what's going on inside the tree determines what gets produced outside the tree. Fig trees have figgy stuff going on inside of them, so they produce figs. They don't produce olives or oranges. Ditto the grapevines. It's impossible to grow figs on a grapevine, because grapevines have grapey stuff going on inside of them. (OK, figgy and grapey aren't real words, but I warned you I'm not a botanist!)

The clue from James is that the inside of the tree is what must be changed by God if a person is going to be transformed. Do you want to produce figs? Then make sure figgy stuff is going on inside of you.

But how does that work? It has to do with storage, Jesus said. Good people store up good things inside.

Think of your inner life as a big computer server. Every day you shove another gigabyte of life experiences into the computer. And depending on what you watch, what you read, the music you listen to, and who you hang with, you are storing up good or bad, true or false, worthy or unworthy ideas and concepts. And your tongue will talk most about whatever you bring up out of the CPU of your heart and mind. "Garbage in, garbage out" is still valid for today.

When I'm working on a special project for someone, I take great care in the materials I put into it. It's fun to see the person's face when I say "It's solid walnut and real gold," rather than "It's pine stained to look like walnut and plastic painted with gold paint." No, I want to put special materials into a project for a special gift.

So why, then, in the most important area of all life—our hearts and minds—do we disregard this teaching from the Master Teacher himself?

Apprenticeship: *Jesus, I have to admit that the bigger problem in my life isn't my tongue, it's my heart. When the hammer of circumstance hits the thumb of my life, what comes out of me falls so short of your glory.*

Lord, help me to be transformed by the renewing of my mind (Romans 12:2). May the words of my mouth and the meditation of my heart be pleasing in your sight, O LORD, my Rock and my Redeemer (Psalm 19:14). Change my heart, so my tongue will speak words of love and life instead of anger and resentment.

STAYING SHARP

As iron sharpens iron, so one man sharpens another.
—Proverbs 27:17

It's easy to take a sharp blade for granted. When blades and tools have a finely honed edge, it can make the woodworking experience an enjoyable one. When a plane is sharp, one pass along the edge of a board creates a smooth ribbon that looks like it just came off a special Christmas package. A long string of waste wood comes off the bowl that's turning on the lathe. And even that stubborn piece of maple submits to the table saw blade.

Unfortunately, as we observed in the previous chapter, the only tool that seems to get sharper with more use is the tongue. But that's for another chapter. When a cutting edge start to dull, it takes the joy out of the project in a hurry. It is also much more dangerous. When a saw blade is dull, we have to push the wood and force it to be cut. Serrated marks are left behind on that piece on the lathe. And instead of ribbons coming off with each pass of the plane, you get jagged cuts that look like Fido has been chewing on your workpiece. Dull blades are their own punishment. You work twice as hard and still end up with shoddy workmanship.

Have you ever met a really sharp Christian? You know, the kind who seems to have real answers to your questions, not simply a warmed-over rehash of what you heard in Sunday school fifteen years ago. The kind of Christian who is comfortable sharing his or her faith without it coming across as pretentious or phony. The kind who seems to have an inner peace and power with them wherever he or she may go. The sharp kind.

When you meet sharp Christ-followers, you can count on two things:

1. They've made a consistent effort to stay sharp.

2. They didn't get sharp overnight!

The good news is that when a blade has lost its bite, the cutting edge can be restored, usually by utilizing a series of progressively finer grit sandpaper or whetstones. Each successive pass of the blade along a sharpening surface can restore even the dullest of tools to a razor edge that will once again cut true. It's no delay to stop and put an edge back on a tool.

If you're like me, once you've sharpened a tool, it's generally the first one you reach for off the workbench. It's that tried-and-true edge that gets the call when I have some serious wood shaping to be done.

Proverbs 27:17 reminds us that one person sharpens another. In other words, fellowship with other Christians can restore us, sharpen us, and give our lives a useful passion, replacing one that has dulled over time. It's so easy to let your spiritual blade lose its edge and become pointless. Just go a few weeks without reading your Bible. Check out of worship with other believers for months at a time. Relegate your prayer life to "God help me" when things aren't going your way. You'll end up as every other tool that's been put up on the shelf, of no use to its owner.

Think of it…

Does Emeril Lagasse enjoy chopping meat with a dull chef's knife?

Do you want your physician performing surgery on you with an edgeless scalpel?

Would the guys from ZZ Top enjoy shaving in the morning with a blunt razor? (OK, maybe they haven't shaved in decades, but I'm sure you get the point!)

Do you really enjoy cutting rock maple on an unsharpened table-saw blade that is full of pitch and dirt?

So why would we try to live the Christian life with a dull heart? Do you want to be used *by* God? Then get useable *for* God. Let him sharpen you. You'll be one of the first tools out of his bag when he needs to accomplish something in someone's life.

Apprenticeship: *Lord, I confess there are times that I try to live on my own, apart from the care and concern of others. I want to be a tool that you will reach for time and again, a sharp instrument in your hands that can accomplish your purposes. But I have allowed the blade of my heart to dull over time, and I am numb to the things of the Spirit. Help me to take the time to allow you put the cutting edge back on my life. Help me to be, as Paul instructed Timothy, "a workman who does not need to be ashamed and who correctly handles the word of truth" (2 Timothy 2:15). Take me by the handle and put me in the best position to sharpen me. Use the abrasiveness of circumstances and other people to hone me, that I might once again know the joy of being a useful tool in the hands of the Master Carpenter.*

JESUS JIG

What you have heard from me, keep as the pattern of sound teaching, with faith and love in Christ Jesus.

—2 Timothy 1:13

Do not conform any longer to the pattern of this world, but be transformed by the renewing of your mind. Then you will be able to test and approve what God's will is—his good, pleasing and perfect will.

—Romans 12:2

While I've made small items for charity auctions, and have made many gifts over the years, I've rarely been paid for any of my woodworking ventures. I don't remember how I got the job, but somehow I got hired to make lids for coffee jars for a coffee bean store just off the boardwalk in Kemah, Texas.

Seems this woman ran a gourmet coffee bean store where customers could scoop their own blend of beans out of large glass jars that were on shelves on the wall. But the original jar lids were made of heavy glass, and customers had a way of accidentally dropping and breaking them. Someone had tried to make a couple lids out of plywood for her, but the lip on the lids didn't seem to fit right in the jar. Could I help?

I started by purchasing one of the jars so I could get the dimensions right. It would not be a problem to construct the lid, but the woman had twenty eight jars! So instead of trying to freehand cut a circle, I decided to use a jig to mass-produce the lids.

A jig is a device, often handmade, that lets a craftsman perform the same cuts time and again and get the same results. It is well worth the extra time to construct and set up a jig, especially for mass production. Once I figured the dimensions of the lid, it was a snap to use a jig on my band saw and cut out the circular lids. They all came out identical, which is what I wanted. After sanding and staining, I let them air out for a time so they wouldn't transfer any odor to the coffee beans. The woman was pleased, and I made some spending money for Christmas.

It got me to thinking, I wish there was a jig for spiritual applications, something that would make my life turn out like Jesus every time. A "What Would Jesus Do?" jig that would guarantee a perfect result each time.

Alas, I have yet to find a Jesus jig. There's nothing that guarantees that I will live a sinless life. In fact, other than for Jesus, living without sin is impossible. The apostle Paul reminds us that the carnal mind is set against God and cannot obey him. There is one particular jig out there, the pattern of the world (Romans 12:2) and if I conform to it, I won't like the end result.

But there is another pattern to follow, a jig we need in the workshop of our heart, the example of Jesus himself. It's hard to answer the question, "WWJD?" if I don't "KWJD" (KNOW What Jesus Did). To do this, I must immerse myself in reading about his life over and over. Paul said we would be transformed by the renewing of our mind. This happens as we read and internalize the Scriptures on a daily basis. Jesus becomes our pattern to follow, and if we follow him faithfully, we may be able to say as Paul told his apprentice, Timothy, "Follow me as I follow Jesus."

Somehow, faith comes by hearing the Word of God. When's the last time you rose early, pulled out your Bible, and actually read aloud the words?

Remember those great Looney Tunes cartoons of yesteryear? I especially enjoyed the Roadrunner and Wile E. Coyote. The scheming coyote (who must've had an uncle who worked for the Acme mail order company) was always falling off cliffs and leaving exact impressions of himself in the ground where he landed. Or he would get trapped behind a wall, and when he would break through the wall, he would leave a hole shaped exactly like his body.

Truth is, I was born trapped behind a wall of sin, and over the years, I added to the wall, brick upon brick, every time I fell short of keeping God's law perfectly. There was no way for me to get over or under the wall. No hope for escape. But the Father knew my dilemma, and so he dropped Jesus over the wall to be in my space with me. And in showing us the way to the Father, Jesus broke through the wall of sin, leaving a Jesus-shaped hole that looks identical to a man hanging on a cross. For us to be able to exit the room of sin, we too must take on the shape and size of Jesus. Once we do, we are freed from the bondage of failures, and WWJD? becomes more than just a bracelet we wear as a fashion statement. It becomes a way of life.

Apprenticeship: *Jesus, I want you to be my jig, my pattern, so that my life will turn out like yours time and time again. I'm not perfect, Lord—you and I both know that. But I want to develop the pattern of walking like you, so that when temptations come, I might look a little more like you each time. Renew my mind in you daily, that I might take on your shape, your size, and your dimensions. Then I'll be able to pass from behind the walls of habitual sin into the freedom of the Father, because I will look like you.*

Materials

For no one can lay any foundation other than the one already laid, which is Jesus Christ. If any man builds on this foundation using gold, silver, costly stones, wood, hay or straw, his work will be shown for what it is, because the Day will bring it to light. It will be revealed with fire, and the fire will test the quality of each man's work.

—1 Corinthians 3:11-13

If you want to build a ship, don't drum up people together to collect wood and don't assign them tasks and work, but rather teach them to long for the endless immensity of the sea.[1]

—Antoine de Saint-Exupéry

Solomon sent this message to Hiram king of Tyre:
"Send me cedar logs as you did for my father David when you sent him cedar to build a palace to live in. Now I am about to build a temple for the Name of the LORD my God and to dedicate it to him . . . . The temple I am going to build will be great, because our God is greater than all other gods. But who is able to build a temple for him, since the heavens, even the highest heavens, cannot contain him? Who then am I to build a temple for him, except as a place to burn sacrifices before him?"

—2 Chronicles 2:3-6

The only really good place to buy lumber is at a store where the lumber has already been cut and attached together in the form of furniture, finished, and put inside boxes.[2]

—Dave Barry

I will give you thanks, for you answered me;
    you have become my salvation.
The stone the builders rejected
    has become the capstone;
the LORD has done this,
    and it is marvelous in our eyes.

—Psalm 118:21-23

ACORNS

He told them another parable: "The kingdom of heaven is like a mustard seed, which a man took and planted in his field. Though it is the smallest of all your seeds, yet when it grows, it is the largest of garden plants and becomes a tree, so that the birds of the air come and perch in its branches."

—Matthew 13:31-32

"So watch yourselves. If your brother sins, rebuke him, and if he repents, forgive him. If he sins against you seven times in a day, and seven times comes back to you and says, 'I repent,' forgive him."

The apostles said to the Lord, "Increase our faith!"

He replied, "If you have faith as small as a mustard seed, you can say to this mulberry tree, 'Be uprooted and planted in the sea,' and it will obey you."

—Luke 17:3-6

Automatic weapon fire in the suburbs is uncommon enough that when I heard it in the middle of the night one fall, I sat up straight in bed, heart pounding. The rat-a-tat sound was coming from right outside our bedroom window, and it sounded like empty shells were hitting the roof.

They were. Acorn shells, that is. The big oak tree in my front yard was attacking my house.

I am blessed to have five large, old growth trees in my yard. (My Houston suburb, Kingwood, is known as the "livable forest.") The oaks shed acorns from year to year, but this past year was a banner year for the trees, which happens every few years. Mature oak trees can produce between two thousand and three thousand acorns a year. I think the oak by our bedroom must have broken a record. The ground around the drip line of the tree was saturated with acorns three and four deep. Whether it was the amount of rainfall or the nutrients all coming together, I don't know. I only know that the squirrels and blue jays were treating our front yard like a fast-food drive-through.

But beyond the neighborhood zoo lining up for feeding time at the Poland house, another critter was getting its fill. Beetles laid their seeds inside the acorns before they became mature, and many of the acorns were destroyed that way. A telltale sign—a tiny hole—could be seen in the side of numerous acorns where the bugs had dug in and made a home for themselves.

Scientists say that the odds of one acorn becoming an oak tree are about one in 10,000. That number shocked me. I would've thought the yield would be much greater.

What does all of this have to do with woodworking, you ask? Plenty. It helps explain why oak is more expensive to work with than pine, for starters. It's also a good reminder that, as woodworkers and carpenters, we need to be concerned about the earth's resources. We need to recycle lumber when we can and we should support reforestation efforts.

There is great meaning in the parable that Jesus taught. Jesus' disciples were confronted with seemingly impossible instructions: to forgive over and over again. They would have taken his admonition to forgive repeatedly to mean that forgiveness should be extended to others in an unlimited way. That would take much more faith than they possessed. "Increase our faith!" they said.

Jesus, however, didn't offer to do that. Instead, he reminded them that from the littlest seeds of hopeful belief, great things can happen.

Ever watch people walk down the aisle of your church to pray or make a decision for Christ? Maybe you caught yourself saying, "Well, that won't last. It's just an emotional decision. They're just young, and they'll get over it." Which one of you honored God—the one who responded in faith with mustard-seed faith, or the one who self-righteously dismissed the notion that anything great could ever come from an act of devotion so small?

Acorns are huge compared to mustard seeds. If you have a drill bit as small as one-sixteenth of an inch, that's a little bigger than a mustard seed, which comes in at one-twentieth of an inch. Yet that seed can grow into a mustard tree, like the acorn can mature into an oak tree. All it takes is time and nutrition.

Ultimately, it's up to you. The care of your seed of faith is your responsibility, not that of your spouse or your minister. You've got to nourish it by planting it in the fertile soil of your heart. Water it daily with God's Word. Warm it with the light of truth. Protect it from the enemy through prayer. And when the seed matures into a fully-grown tree, give the fruit of your life away.

Maybe there's a tree of hurt in your way today. Perhaps it's something much bigger, like an entire mountain of forgiveness that you need to extend to someone who has wronged you. According to Jesus, the tree and the mountain can both be dealt with the same way—by faith. Great results aren't dependent upon our having Pikes Peak–sized faith—a granule of faith will do. We exercise the faith, he produces the results, which are always greater than what we thought possible.

Apprenticeship: *Forgive me, Lord, for my cynicism and lack of belief. I confess that my faith is not only small, but rusty and underutilized. We both know my unforgiving spirit toward others is a major cause of my lack of faith. Help me, Master Carpenter, that as I grow to forgive others, just like you've forgiven me, my faith might mature into something that would bear much fruit for your glory.*

ROTTEN BOARDS

A heart at peace gives life to the body,
but envy rots the bones.

—Proverbs 14:30

Even a new house needs an inspection from time to time to identify problems. A termite inspection is always warranted. Moisture barriers don't last forever. Rot and deterioration can come in many forms, as I found out the hard way.

The previous owner of my house had built a patio cover, really an arbor of sorts, long before we moved in. Constructed entirely of wood and connected to the back of the house, it allowed just enough sunlight to allow potted plants to grow, and just enough shade to keep the blazing Texas sun off when we grill outdoors. But it trapped leaves and pine needles and required frequent cleaning, which was a pain. It was beginning to discolor, and I began to wonder what it might be doing to the fascia boards of the house to which it was attached.

When we grew tired of the cover and the seemingly endless supply of leaves it supported, we decided to tear it down. I suspected there would be a little rot behind it, but I wasn't prepared for what I saw. Over time, the rain coming down the roof had run down between the fascia boards of the house and the beams of the patio cover, down into places that never saw sun or wind to dry them out. As a result, any place where the patio cover touched the house, the fascia boards and soffits needed to be replaced. Soft doesn't begin to describe the wood I found there. I could literally take my finger and punch holes in two-by-eight boards!

Rot is one of the worst enemies your house has, and it's also one of the worst enemies your heart has. The danger is that things can look so solid on the outside, but rot is working away where you don't see it until it is too late. According to Proverbs, envy is one of those things that causes rot in a life, bringing damage to the deepest parts of a person. Envy occurs when we see what someone else has and we want it, but we want it without doing what they did to get it. Envy is a deliberate shortcut.

Compared to the big bad sins like murder or rape, envy doesn't get much attention, just like one rotting board on the side of a house doesn't sound so bad. It won't bring down the house, right? My envy doesn't hurt anyone else, right? I can't be convicted in a court of law for being envious. Yet in the proverb above, envy is said to be a cause of spiritual rot.

Envy is one of the seven deadly sins, and it was because of the envy of others that Jesus was arrested (Matthew 27:18). The religious leaders envied the power and authority Jesus had; they envied the way large crowds would follow him; and they envied the miracles he performed. Envy led them to try and trap him in his own words. When that didn't work, it drove them to get rid of him. They delivered him up, not only to death, but also to their own pride and self-importance and the need to be in charge, the need to have the center stage, in order to feed the rot of their bones.

How can you tell if you've got some envy rot behind what others see in you? Perform a heart inspection: Do you look at others that have something you don't have and gossip or talk about them sarcastically? Often we do this because we lack something (the looks, the success, the physique, the toys, etc.), and we try to build ourselves up by spouting hurtful words about the other person. Ultimately, envy is our way of judging God to be wrong in allowing someone else to have what they have.

In Psalm 73, a choir director named Asaph describes his envy of the wicked, people who seem to have no struggles (v. 4) as they increase in wealth (v. 12). Asaph's envy stemmed from his own insecurity, but when he began to worship, he saw the truth. "Whom have I in heaven but you? And earth has nothing I desire besides you," he sang to the Lord in v. 25. When we, like

Asaph, realize our security lies in God and not in the possessions we don't have, we reverse the rotting process in our hearts.

If you find some heart decay behind the boards of your soul, try this for a fix: Begin to pray for and work toward the success of others, particularly your enemies. In doing so, you'll replace the envy-weakened structure of your heart with a strong peace that will bring contentment to your entire being. Don't wait until it feels right to do so, just do it.

Apprenticeship: *O Lord, give me grace to so closely follow you that I cease to envy the prosperity of anyone else, but rather rejoice to honor others before myself. Solidify the rotten parts of my life with the strength of your Word. Help me to worship you in such a way that I am restored and regain your perspective on my life.*

VALUABLE SCRAPS

One day as he was teaching, Pharisees and teachers of the law, who had come from every village of Galilee and from Judea and Jerusalem, were sitting there. And the power of the Lord was present for him to heal the sick. Some men came carrying a paralytic on a mat and tried to take him into the house to lay him before Jesus. When they could not find a way to do this because of the crowd, they went up on the roof and lowered him on his mat through the tiles into the middle of the crowd, right in front of Jesus.

When Jesus saw their faith, he said, "Friend, your sins are forgiven."

The Pharisees and the teachers of the law began thinking to themselves, "Who is this fellow who speaks blasphemy? Who can forgive sins but God alone?"

Jesus knew what they were thinking and asked, "Why are

you thinking these things in your hearts? Which is easier: to say, 'Your sins are forgiven,' or to say, 'Get up and walk'? But that you may know that the Son of Man has authority on earth to forgive sins . . . ." He said to the paralyzed man, "I tell you, get up, take your mat and go home." Immediately he stood up in front of them, took what he had been lying on and went home praising God. Everyone was amazed and gave praise to God. They were filled with awe and said, "We have seen remarkable things today."

—Luke 5:17-26

After finishing a project, invariably I will have some scrap material left over. These are usually cut-offs, or perhaps pieces that I cut twice and they were still too short! Not quite enough cedar left for that Adirondack chair. Walnut in 8/4 thickness, but not big enough for a box. A chunk of cherry. A piece of purpleheart. These and other scraps go into a bin that I built because it's really hard for me to throw anything away. I hoard these pieces until they threaten to take over my garage.

Of course, even if I were to purchase more lumber, it would be hard to match the consistency of the color and the grain to the scraps that I already have. But I save most scraps, believing that all lumber has value. I can use that purpleheart and cherry as inlay material. The walnut could be a pull for a drawer or a fan. Perhaps I can coax a small planter box out of that cedar.

Very few "white collar" vocations existed in Jesus' time. Most people performed vast amounts of manual labor simply to have food and shelter each day. A paralyzed man would not be able to do carpentry, or plow a field, or catch a fish. His worth to the people around him would be almost nil.

Jesus lived and taught in a day when people were often considered scrap material. The lame and leprous were the street dust of society, and their lives bore the sandal marks of the oblivious religious community who piously walked over them. The Pharisees were more concerned with matters of the law than matters of the lame, so they had ignored this paralyzed man, discarding him like wood pulp.

The response of the Master Carpenter, however, was to reclaim this limp-limbed man from the scrap bin and restore him in two ways: He healed the man's body, and he healed the man's heart.

"Friend, your sins are forgiven," Jesus told the man. His words must have seemed like a shock to the religious leaders, who were desensitized to the lame man's pain and suffering. Who was this man on the mat, that the Rabbi should call him friend? At the same time, his words probably sounded like a welcome appraisal by a fine antique dealer to a man who had been discarded as a worthless piece of junk. His body and his heart restored, this cast-off would never again doubt his value. The Master Carpenter had touched him, not because he was beautiful or rich or could do more work than any other man in a single day. No, he received a touch from Jesus simply because he was.

Have you been asking Jesus for a physical healing of some sort? He can do it, there's no doubt. But don't stop there. Ask him for a healing of your heart as well.

Are there people around you who are regarded as "scraps" by the rest of society? That person at work who doesn't understand boundaries? That child in the wheelchair with severe developmental issues? That single mother struggling to raise a family without support? These people are waiting for your touch. Stretch out *your* hand, even if theirs isn't reaching out. You both might encounter a healing of sorts in the process.

Apprenticeship: *Lord, it is hard to for me to see myself as you see me. I try every day to prove my worth to the people around me, but you established my ultimate value at the cross, not at my place of employment. So help me this day to live in your liberating power, knowing that I am a person of great worth and value to you. Help me to see others in the same way, and serve as your tool of compassion in their lives today. May I be an agent of your healing power to another.*

HARD WOOD

Therefore say: "This is what the Sovereign LORD says: I will gather you from the nations and bring you back from the countries where you have been scattered, and I will give you back the land of Israel again."

They will return to it and remove all its vile images and detestable idols. I will give them an undivided heart and put a new spirit in them; I will remove from them their heart of stone and give them a heart of flesh. Then they will follow my decrees and be careful to keep my laws. They will be my people, and I will be their God. But as for those whose hearts are devoted to their vile images and detestable idols, I will bring down on their own heads what they have done, declares the Sovereign LORD.

—Ezekiel 11:17-21

What is the hardest wood to work with? Some exotic species from a rain forest? A near-extinct variety from Siberia? Or perhaps it's the rock maple from your neck of the woods? What kind of wood makes your hundred-dollar saw blade stop dead in its tracks?

Do you give up? None of the above. The hardest wood on the planet is petrified wood.

Petrified wood is really a fossil that was once alive. When a piece of wood is buried under a layer of sediment, mineral-rich water flows through the sediment and deposits minerals into the cells of the wood. Over time, and in the absence of oxygen, the organic matter in the wood decomposes and is replaced volume-for-volume by silica and other minerals that preserve its form and woody structure. Inorganic material slowly replaces organic matter with such detail that you can identify the original tree.

Oddly enough, while petrified wood is harder than steel, if you hit it just right, it will shatter because it is also very brittle.

In the Book of Ezekiel, God's people were a lot like pieces of petrified wood. The parts of their hearts that had been alive for God had slowly ebbed away, and their soft, living hearts had been replaced by hearts of stone—cold, unmoving, and dead.

Evidently, the big reason for this was idolatry. God's people had slowly substituted the worship of the living God for the worship of "vile images and detestable idols." The idols they worshipped probably were made of wood, stone, or metal. And since we inevitably become like that which we worship, their hearts were as cold, dead, and unmoving as that which they worshipped.

Chances are good that you have never bowed down to some Tiki god sitting on a shelf in your home. You've probably never prayed to a painting on the wall, or brought burnt offerings to a bronze statue (although I've served up many a charred meal from the grill to my family!). Yet we are all guilty of idolatry, and here's why: Idolatry is simply choosing anything over God. Period. The early church father Augustine once said, "Idolatry is worshiping anything that ought to be used, or using anything that is meant to be worshiped."

God has created us to worship, and we do it really well if you consider that worship is simply emphasizing the value of something (or someone) else. And it doesn't take much to determine what we worship. Take a look at where you spend your money or your time. Check out what makes your heart beat faster, or where your passion lies. What does your bank account say you are more devoted to than anything else? All these roads lead to the same altar, and we regularly bow down before it and worship. The problem isn't that God has created us to worship. Instead, the real dilemma is that many of us worship some really lousy gods that aren't alive. And we become like that which we worship.

With every act of devotion, with every pledge of allegiance to our "little g" god, we slowly replace the organic, living material in our hearts with cold, hard stone. An idol can even be a hobby, such as fishing, bicycling, or (say it ain't so!) even woodworking. We pursue these because they are fun, and they add enjoyment to our lives. But when we try to make them life itself, they eventually leave us empty and defrauded. In fact, we create the idol, but it ends up devouring us.

Sometimes we confuse the matter and get our work and play confused. Leland Ryken, a professor at Wheaton University, once said that we worship our work, work at our play, and play at our worship.

Fortunately, God has a remedy for petrified hearts. He promises that as his people return to him, he will remove their heart of stone and once again give them a heart of flesh. A heart that is beating and alive. A heart that is concerned with the things God is concerned about. A heart that knows the truth and tells the truth. A heart that breaks at the things that break God's heart.

Apprenticeship: *Master Surgeon, I don't know when it first began, but slowly I have allowed the very life of my heart to ebb away and be replaced by cold, hard stone. I feel trapped under the sediment of sin, and I feel like I'm slowly losing the things I care for most. My heart rarely beats in time with yours anymore.*

But you are able to open me up with precision and skill and replace that which is dead to you with something that is alive to you. I confess, my life only has value as long as it has something valuable as its object. I return to you, my true treasure, and willingly place myself on the table in your surgical suite. Perform this transplant now, O Lord, before my spiritual life slips away even further. Then I will know and enjoy the true life I was meant to live. Then I will worship you alone, and will become like you alone.

JOINERY

"My sheep listen to my voice; I know them, and they follow me. I give them eternal life, and they shall never perish; no one can snatch them out of my hand. My Father, who has given them to me, is greater than all; no one can snatch them out of my Father's hand. I and the Father are one."

—John 10:27-30

Shaping the wood is fun. I love making sawdust. But after shaping, something has to happen to it. Very few woodworking projects I've ever done consisted of one piece of wood. Usually they entail many pieces, put together by different joints and glue.

Butt joints are the simplest, but they are also the first to fail unless reinforced by dowels or biscuits. Rabbet joints are stronger, and lap joints have their place when making frame and panel doors. My first attempts at mortise and tenon joints for a display frame to hold antique quilts weren't that great looking, but they were definitely stronger than anything else I had ever made.

But the granddaddy of them all is the dovetail joint, and it is by far the strongest and most beautiful way to join two pieces of wood. My hand-cut dovetails still look rather shoddy (I learned the hard way that you can use only so much of that filler stuff in a dovetail joint before it begins to lose its strength), but I've cut some better ones with a router and a dovetail fixture. One test of a skilled cabinet maker's work is to pull a drawer out and admire his dovetails. Hundreds of years later, the joints that were built to last are still holding.

Glue makes a big difference, too. Too much or too little glue can weaken the joint. Just the right amount must be applied, and then the assembly can be clamped up. Even the clamps make a difference. Too much pressure forces too much glue out of the joint, further weakening the piece. Too little pressure doesn't allow the wood pieces to bond with each other.

While you may not have learned anything new about joinery in the last few paragraphs, have you ever considered how you are joined to God?

Some folks are afraid that they are joined to God by the slimmest of butt joints, with a half-drop of glue adhering the two. One wrong move, one sin, and the two pieces are separated. They live their lives in fear, as if their joinery—their connection to God depends on their personal performance. They may have walked the aisle several times, prayed to receive Christ on multiple occasions, and have even been baptized more times than the preacher at the annual church festival's dunking booth. But they still live in fear that one day they'll lose their salvation, or at the very least so totally displease the Lord that he'll turn his back on them at the very end of the age.

Take your right hand and open it, palm up. Now take your left hand, palm down, and lay it on top, perpendicular to your right hand. Curl your fingers around your hands. Looks somewhat like a lap joint, doesn't it?

When you receive the gift of eternal life, you are put into the hand of Christ, and the Father has his hand wrapped around the hand of Christ. No one— not even you—can snatch you out of the Father's hand. He has given you *eternal* life—not life for a day or a month or three years, until you blow it by sinning. (If it was something you could lose, it wouldn't be called *eternal* life, would it?) It will last forever. There's nothing you can do to undo the bond.

Think of it this way: If you could do something to lose your salvation, then evidently you are saved by both your faith and your good works. And that runs contrary to Scripture. Ephesians 2:8-9 says, "For it is by grace you have been saved, through faith—and this not from yourselves, it is the gift of God—not by works, so that no one can boast."

Imagine trying to balance the scales of your life. Can you really ever do enough good to outweigh the bad your life has produced? I couldn't begin to do that. Your life would be in constant flux, up one moment and down the next. Is that really the spiritual, abundant life that Jesus came to give?

Furthermore, to say that you could lose your salvation by sinning is to say that the blood of Jesus was only sufficient to cover some of your sins, not all of them. It is to say that Jesus wasn't good enough, holy enough, strong enough, to save you. Is that really how you feel about Christ's sacrifice for you?

No, you and I have been joined by the Master Carpenter himself to the one who is the Ancient of Days, who was here long before we got here, and who will be here long after we have passed off this earth. You may not always *feel* close to God. It doesn't matter. God *is* close to you, as close as two pieces of wood joined together by the glue of Christ's strength.

Incidentally, a dovetail joint can be made by interlocking your fingers together, palms toward each other. Looks like you're ready to pray, doesn't it? Maybe that's the real secret of feeling joined to God on an ongoing basis. Prayer drives away the doubt when we question if we are really joined to the Lord. It connects us to God in ways that no other spiritual discipline does.

Apprenticeship: *I thank you, Master Carpenter, that your spiritual joinery is dependent on you, not me, and you know how to make joints last forever. I know I am saved by faith, by your grace, not by my good works. Please forgive me for the times I try to live trusting in my good works, not in your grace. Help me to be a living example to the world of one who is permanently joined to God by the glue of Jesus Christ.*

110

MEASURE TWICE, CUT ONCE

My dear brothers, take note of this: Everyone should be
quick to listen, slow to speak and slow to become angry, for
man's anger does not bring about the righteous life that
God desires.

—James 1:19-20

was in a hurry. While converting a wet bar into an entertainment center in
our den (a Baptist minister has little use for a wet bar if he wants to stay
employed for very long!), I was taking several measurements for the shelv-
ing. I made my cuts outside, to avoid sawdust inside the house. But after a
few hours, I was getting tired and wanted to hurry and finish. I took a meas-
urement, went outside and made the cut, then brought the board back into
the house to dry fit it. It was too short. So I remeasured the space and went
back outside. Then, for some unknown reason (I think the angel of "duh"
encamped about my forehead and lo, I was very confused) I went back to the

table saw and *cut the same board again.*

It was still too short.

Of course, it was my last board, and I had to go back to the lumberyard for more wood.

"Measure twice, cut once" is probably the first axiom any budding woodworker learns. The truth is, most woodworking is all about setting up for the cut. Measuring, setting adjustments on the saw, measuring again, double-checking the saw settings for accuracy, and then finally making the cut. It's just that it's so much fun to rev up the saw and shape the wood that sometimes I get ahead of myself.

Perhaps "Measure twice, cut once" should be a principle we apply to the words that come out of our mouths, as well. You would think we would learn early in life to measure our words before we say them. To listen to them twice in our mind before we say them once. The results can be catastrophic if we don't. Words cut to the core of who we are, and a lot of damage can be created in a hurry when our tongue runs at a high RPM.

The problems I've seen in every church in which I've served weren't usually problems of theology, but problems of anatomy. So often it turned out to be a three-inch muscle—the tongue—that could bring down a six-foot-tall man time and time again. And as we saw in the chapter on "The Hitting the Nail on the Head," it's really a problem of the heart.

Have you ever considered how you might measure your words? Here are some guidelines for gauging your speech: Don't be hasty—think about what's necessary. We're taught to never turn a power tool on unless we know exactly what it is going to do when the blade starts turning. Consider the effect of what you're about to say. In the scenario above, I was in a hurry. Sometimes in a hurry to make our point with someone, in our haste to justify ourselves with our words, we come across as short and defensive with others.

Make sure you've got the right tool for the right job. Don't use a radial arm saw with a twelve-inch blade when a small coping saw will do. Sometimes with our speech we exaggerate when trying to make our point. (Using the words "always" and "never" are good examples—save yourself some grief with your spouse before you say "You *always* do this." or "You *never* do that.")

Check your volume, too. Does the person you are communicating with have to wear OSHA-approved ear protection while listening to you? Screaming and yelling to make your point may make you feel better in the short run, but it also gives you more to be sorry for later, and causes damage that another may never get over. Use a gentle answer when responding to others.

Perform a neck-up check-up and a cardio-exam. Is the problem really the problem? Or is your speech just a symptom of a bigger problem? Are you really ready to confront the other person? Or are you lashing out in anger? If any part of you relishes the idea of putting another person in their place with your words, then you're just not ready to confront them, plain and simple. Do your words give life and edify, or do they tear others down?

Apprenticeship: *God who gave me two ears and one mouth, I don't want to measure my words, because if I'm totally honest, they often have cut other people down. My tongue has sliced through the veneer of people into the heartwood of their lives, causing them hurt and pain. My unmeasured words have also brought reproach to your name.*

Slow me down, Father. May I not be so enamored with the sound of my own voice that I rev its motor into life before I'm sure what the blade of my tongue will do and where it will go. You desire that I speak with a righteous tongue. May that desire be fulfilled as I allow you to change my heart.

GLUING IT UP

So the LORD God caused the man to fall into a deep sleep; and while he was sleeping, he took one of the man's ribs and closed up the place with flesh. Then the LORD God made a woman from the rib he had taken out of the man, and he brought her to the man.

The man said,

"This is now bone of my bones and flesh of my flesh; she shall be called 'woman,' for she was taken out of man.'"

For this reason a man will leave his father and mother and

be united to his wife, and they will become one flesh.

—Genesis 2:21-24

've never used epoxy in woodworking. I can see where someone might have to use an oil base adhesive if they're working on a boat or some other project that needs to be waterproof, but the crafts and small furniture that I make just require a good bond with basic yellow wood glue. If the joint is made right, the glue does its job and holds the pieces tight.

Gluing up boards for tabletops is lots of fun. I typically use a biscuit joiner, but I've dabbled with dowels and even a tongue and groove in the past. It's just that the biscuit joiner makes the process so easy. Once the biscuit slots are cut in the right places, a little glue secures the biscuit in the slot and the edges of the boards against each other. After being clamped up for even half an hour, the many boards have become one big board, and if glued correctly, it is virtually impossible to separate the pieces. Separation *can* be done, but usually the pieces separate violently in splinters and shards and are unable to be reused.

Oh that it were so simple with marriage, right? Marriage is supposed to be a picture of Christ's love for the church and her love for him. That's one reason why divorce is so harmful—it presents a harmful picture, as if Christ and his bride were together, then violently separated. It subtly tells the world that God's love is not unconditional, that he is not faithful to his bride, and that we might be better off apart from him. When a marriage fails, it leaves the couple with sharp edges, jagged shards of baggage that they carry on to the next relationship.

Ecclesiastes 4:12 says "Though one may be overpowered, two can defend themselves. A cord of three strands is not quickly broken." The Holy Spirit is the glue in a marriage between two Christians. When those two are joined together, wrapped around him, they become a cord of three strands.

Most of my tools are outside in the garage. I do have a small toolbox with a just a few essentials that stays inside the house. That way I don't have to go outside for a simple screwdriver or a pair of pliers. So, just how do you go about gluing up a marriage so that it lasts? Here are some tools for working on your marriage that you might want to take inside the house and keep within reach:

1. **Prayer Pliers**—Praying together on a regular basis with your spouse will cause the two of you to hold tight together when difficult blows are being hammered on your relationship. There is power in agreement together in prayer, and your spouse will have a new respect for you as you pray together, even if you stumble over your words.

2. **Servanthood Screwdriver**—Just like screws hold boards together, the act of servanthood helps bind a husband and wife together. Ephesians 5:21-33 gives some very practical instructions for a healthy marriage. Husbands are to love their wives just like Christ loved the church. How did Jesus do that? He wore a crown of thorns and was crucified in our place. If a man is intent on being the king of his castle, the only crown he can dare wear is a crown of thorns, laying his life down daily in service for his wife.

3. **Laughter Level**—Joy keeps a relationship balanced. When we take ourselves too seriously, we create an atmosphere of tension. You don't have to be a big

joke-teller. Just find the humor in everyday situations and let down your guard with your spouse. By creating a safe atmosphere where joy can be expressed, your relationship will grow to new heights and be on the level.

4. Forgiveness Framer—Once the preferred tool of choice for laying out the rafters of a roof, now a framing square is used mainly to measure and mark larger things such as plywood or bigger lumber. A marriage is a big thing indeed, and the health of a marriage can be measured by how much forgiveness is exercised in the relationship. Holding grudges and recounting past wrongs is a sure sign that the forgiveness framer has been left outside in the garage.

Apprenticeship: *Thank you, Lord, for my spouse. How my marriage needs to be a wholesome picture of your love for the world! Help me bring some helpful tools into my relationship with my spouse, and help me to use them gently to build up our marriage. Glue us up, Lord, and may the bond never be broken.*

USELESS MATERIALS

The word of the LORD came to me: "Son of man, how is the wood of a vine better than that of a branch on any of the trees in the forest? Is wood ever taken from it to make anything useful? Do they make pegs from it to hang things on? And after it is thrown on the fire as fuel and the fire burns both ends and chars the middle, is it then useful for anything? If it was not useful for anything when it was whole, how much less can it be made into something useful when the fire has burned it and it is charred?

"Therefore this is what the Sovereign LORD says: As I have given the wood of the vine among the trees of the forest as fuel for the fire, so will I treat the people living in Jerusalem. I will set my face against them. Although they have come out of the fire, the fire will yet consume them. And when I set my face against them, you will know that I

am the LORD. I will make the land desolate because they
have been unfaithful, declares the Sovereign LORD."

—Ezekiel 15:1-8

Where do you get the lumber for your projects? The first place to look
might be a local lumberyard. But when you want something other than
basic pine, you might have to order it and wait weeks for it to arrive. If
you're fortunate, you might live near a specialty yard where they carry more
exotic woods, especially in useful sizes. Walnut plywood for extra-special cabinetry. Spalted Elm for turning a bowl. And if you're really fortunate, you live
near a sawmill where you can drive right to the site and have your material
cut to a custom size. I've utilized all these alternatives before. But one option
I've never turned to is the vines that grow along my back fence.

A vine is valued for the fruit that it bears, not for the actual woody part of
the vine. I haven't noticed any 2 x 4s made out of grapevine at the lumberyard lately. Have you seen any new homes being constructed out of vine?
Roofing material? Doors? It's hard to imagine hearing a homebuyer saying,
"Yep, I got a real good deal on this corner of suburbia. It comes with a six-
day warranty. Solid vine walls and doors. Gives us a sense of bringing the outdoors right inside with us. And you've got to love the aroma!"

Here in Ezekiel 15, God, through Ezekiel, describes his children as a vine that no longer bears fruit. Without fruit, the vine is totally useless, except as kindling for a fire.

The parallel is obvious. We are called to bear fruit, and we can't do that by ourselves. And without the Lord, we won't bear the fruit he calls us to bear. Once it is determined that we're not going to be fruitful, well, what else are we good for? If we're not careful, we could build our lives with useless materials (such as a fruitless vine) and give ourselves over to trivial pursuits instead of choosing to live for eternity.

Imagine your workbench covered with everything you own, everything you cherish, everything you've sought after in your life. (For some of us, the idea of our workbench totally covered isn't so hard to imagine—the top of our workbenches haven't seen the light of day in a long time!) It holds everything you've accumulated, both possessions and character qualities.

Each item on the workbench has a price tag, and you probably know exactly what you paid for many of them. You got that dovetail jig on sale at a woodworking show, but it still cost some serious coin. Your (flannel shirt was a bargain at the local discount store. But the bench also holds your car (OK, it's a huge workbench!), and you know that wasn't cheap. And is that a boat over on the corner of your workbench? A pretty penny you paid for it, no?

There are also some other items to be found on the workbench. Love. Justice. Faithfulness. Mercy. Forgiveness. A relationship with God. Your relationship with others. And these items also have price tags attached to them.

Question is, which items have the higher price attached to them? Which ones do you value more?

Before we come to faith in Christ, we adhere to one particular economic system: that of the world. We value what the magazines and television and movies and the Internet tell us to value. Looks. Possessions. Power. Prestige.

But when we come to faith in Christ, it is as if Jesus changes the price tags on all those items on the workbench. What once passed for valuable is now so much vine-material. And what we once considered worthy of little attention is now—priceless.

Are you being faithful to give yourself over to the most valuable things in life? When you get to the end of your life (and you will, by the way!) will you have something more than a vine-house to show for it?

Apprentice: *Master Carpenter, I see that you are also the Master Economist, and I need a class in heaven's Economics 101. I confess I have held onto unworthy things in my life, and they have made me unworthy. I've chased after all that the vines of this life have to offer, and have found that they make shoddy building material. Help me set my focus on that which is truly valuable in the kingdom. I want to be fruitful. And I know that the only way it will happen is to allow you to change the price tags on my workbench.*

THAT WHICH COST ME NOTHING

On that day Gad went to David and said to him, "Go up and build an altar to the LORD on the threshing floor of Araunah the Jebusite." So David went up, as the LORD had commanded through Gad. When Araunah looked and saw the king and his men coming toward him, he went out and bowed down before the king with his face to the ground.

Araunah said, "Why has my lord the king come to his servant?" "To buy your threshing floor," David answered, "so I can build an altar to the LORD, that the plague on the people may be stopped."

Araunah said to David, "Let my lord the king take whatever pleases him and offer it up. Here are oxen for the burnt offering, and here are threshing sledges and ox yokes for the wood. O king, Araunah gives all this to the king." Araunah also said to him, "May the LORD your God accept you."

But the king replied to Araunah, "No, I insist on paying you for it. I will not sacrifice to the LORD my God burnt offerings that cost me nothing."

"So David bought the threshing floor and the oxen and paid fifty shekels of silver for them. David built an altar to the LORD there and sacrificed burnt offerings and fellowship offerings. Then the LORD answered prayer in behalf of the land, and the plague on Israel was stopped.

—2 Samuel 24:18-25

Two threshing sledges—five shekels
Two ox yokes—seven shekels
Two oxen—thirty eight shekels
The joy of worshipping the Lord—priceless.

From the beginning of Scripture, we see example after example of God-followers who were challenged to give their best to the Lord. In the first offering recorded (Genesis 4:2-5), Cain brought just "some" of the fruits of his garden, but his brother Abel brought fat portions from the firstborn of his livestock. God was pleased with Abel's offering, but not so happy about Cain's. The point is not that God prefers animal sacrifice over home-grown offerings (and some of you guys thought this was a license to eat meat and eschew green vegetables!), but that Abel offered his best to God while Cain only "tipped" God like you might do a waiter at a restaurant.

At other times God's people gave the best they had to worship and honor the Lord. Second Chronicles 3–4 describes the temple that was built during Solomon's reign and the magnificent materials that were used in its construction. Walls with jewels, doors overlaid with gold, an altar of bronze, and brilliantly-colored curtains of fine linen, all made of the finest resources available at the time. The temple cost a great deal in terms of money and time, but was it worth it? The simple answer is, "Yes." When the temple was dedicated, God's presence was so thick among the people that "the priests could not perform their service because of the cloud, for the glory of the LORD filled the temple of God," (2 Chronicles 5:13-14). Great sacrifice yields great worship.

And that's what King David meant years before, when he turned down Araunah's offer to supply all that David needed to worship. "I will not sacrifice to the Lord my God burnt offerings that cost me nothing," he said. We should offer God our very best, because ultimately he's the only one who deserves it.

Have you ever done that on a project? Or do you tend to look at your work and say, "That'll pass. That's close enough. It'll do until something better comes along."

Instead, why not autograph your work with excellence? Why not use the finest materials, giving the best of your time, at the greatest cost?

Now I can just hear some of you aspiring perfectionists out there saying, "But it's never good enough. I can't do it perfectly."

Excellence isn't perfection, which implies never making a mistake or an oversight. Not a one of us is capable of perfection. There's always someone else who can do it better.

Excellence is simply doing the best you can with the materials you have. It will cost, to be sure. But it honors the Lord. Every time. Colossians 3:23 says, "Whatever you do, work at it with *all* your heart, as working for the Lord, not for men."

David could have taken the easy path that day in Aranuah's field. But he knew that great worship needed great sacrifice. And the rest of the story is just as interesting. Years later, when David's son Solomon built the temple, he built it right on top of Aranuah's threshing floor, where David had been obedient to offer his best to God.

About 1000 years later, God wanted to express his great love for the people of this planet, that they might turn to him. Realizing that a great love demands a great sacrifice, he offered up that which was dearest to him—the most excellent of gifts—his only Son. And at Calvary, a great sacrifice yielded great worship. Only this time, it wasn't the one offering up the sacrifice who was doing the worshipping. God gave up Jesus as a sacrifice that we might worship him in a great manner.

Apprenticeship: *A purple robe—two denarii*
A crown of thorns—one-sixteenth of a denarius
Two crossbeams—one-fourth of a denarius
Three nails—one-eighth of a denarius
The Lamb of God, giving his best for me? Priceless.

Finishing

Consider it pure joy, my brothers, whenever you face trials of many kinds, because you know that the testing of your faith develops perseverance. Perseverance must finish its work so that you may be mature and complete, not lacking anything.

—James 1:2-4

Many men build as cathedrals were built, the part nearest the ground finished; but that part which soars toward heaven, the turrets and the spires, forever incomplete.[1]

—Henry Ward Beecher

I have fought the good fight, I have finished the race, I have kept the faith.

—2 Timothy 4:7

Do each job as if it is your last act on earth, but work on it as if you have eternity to finish.

—Unknown

Now finish the work, so that your eager willingness to do it may be matched by your completion of it, according to your means.

—2 Corinthians 8:11

We shall neither fail nor falter; we shall not weaken or tire . . . give us the tools and we will finish the job.[2]

—Winston Churchill

When he had received the drink, Jesus said, "It is finished." With that, he bowed his head and gave up his spirit.

—John 19:30

THE SANDING STATION

Then the word of the LORD came to Elijah: "Leave here, turn eastward and hide in the Kerith Ravine, east of the Jordan. You will drink from the brook, and I have ordered the ravens to feed you there."

—1 Kings 17:2-4

Mention the word *sanding* to anyone and you're liable to get a frown followed by a rolling of the eyes. No one likes to sand, but the truth is, we won't be pleased with any project until we do it.

My eyes and nose protest violently every time I sand. Whether it's aggressively removing unwanted material at the belt sander with a sixty-grit paper that wants to peel back my skin as easily as the wood, or a light hand sanding with a 600-grit wet-dry paper, I never enjoy the process. And sanding can be tedious, too. I once made the mistake of sanding through a beautiful veneer, leaving a terribly unsightly mark in the work piece. It was totally ruined and eventually resigned to the scrap pile.

Everyone agrees that the best sanding should start with a heavier grit paper and work upward to the finer grits, perhaps even finishing with steel wool. Though it's hard work, I'll admit it is very satisfying to run my hand over a tabletop that has gone through all the stages of sanding. It doesn't even resemble the rough-cut wood I started with.

Consider what happens at the beginning of our journey of faith with the Lord. We much more resemble rough-cut lumber rather than a fully finished product. We've got plenty of jagged edges, places where others can pick up splinters as they come in contact with us. There's plenty of abrasiveness in our words that can rub people the wrong way. Sharp corners in our attitudes can slice open wounds in others, even unintentionally.

The prophet Elijah learned a thing or two about sanding. In 1 Kings 17, God sent him to the Kerith Ravine, east of the Jordan. He had to get his water from a brook, and the only food he had to eat was takeout—whatever the ravens brought him. (Ravens are scavengers, so it's safe to assume Elijah wasn't getting gourmet fare!) Compounding his troubles, the Lord next sent him to the home of a destitute widow whose pantry was empty.

Then God did a miraculous thing through Elijah. He caused the widow's cooking supplies of flour and oil to continuously multiply, and she had enough to sustain them day after day. At one point, the widow's son became ill and died, and yet God used Elijah to resuscitate the boy and restore life to him.

The Hebrew word *Kerith* means "cut." When Elijah was obedient to go to the Kerith Ravine, God began to cut on him. Cutting away the dead wood of self-reliance. Sanding down the attitudes rotted by sin. Trimming away the splinters of self-righteousness. Slicing open the infections of bitterness and allowing the poison of unforgiveness to run out, prompting real healing.

And after God had cut on Elijah in that Kerith Ravine, he was able to use the prophet in these miraculous ways. Interestingly enough, the chapter begins with Elijah known as "Elijah the Tishbite." By the time Elijah is in the recovery room after the spiritual surgery, he is referred to as "Elijah, the man of God." And this is the same Elijah who later stood before the prophets of Baal and called down fire from heaven.

But you can't call down fire from heaven until God has cut on you for a while. And so the Carpenter begins to work with us. He may begin with a planer, gradually shaving off uneven places on the wood's surface. Once the wood is finished at the planer, work at the sanding station is just beginning. God may use the grit of difficult circumstances and discouraging moments to smooth our lives. A disappointing performance review at work, an illness, a fender-bender in the car. All these common events can feel like so much sandpaper on our lives.

And yet, when the Master Carpenter takes us to the sanding station, the results can be beautiful. Have you submitted to the ways of God in your life concerning trials? Ever consider that you can't be all you want to be without being sanded down? Don't worry; the hand of the Master Carpenter is loving. He knows just when to stop the sanding and when to begin applying the finish coats.

Here's a thought: We grow more like Christ when we are forced to love others that we find difficult to love. Losing your patience with that coworker? Did you let some angry words slip out at that other driver on the freeway? Welcome to the sanding station. But then, how will you ever learn patience if no one's around to test yours?

Apprenticeship: *Lord, I don't like it when you cut and sand on my life. There. I've said it, and you knew it even before I said it.*

But I do want to be used by you to accomplish great things. So I choose to submit to your ways today. I trust your hand to be loving, and I believe that you know just how much sanding I can take to make me reflect the image of Jesus. Instead of running from irritating gritty circumstances today, help me embrace them as agents of change that you bring into my life.

A FRESH COAT

Blessed is he whose transgressions are forgiven, whose sins are covered.

—Psalm 32:1

Above all, love each other deeply, because love covers over a multitude of sins.

—1 Peter 4:8

Painting is one of the least expensive things you can do to bring a fresh look to your home. New colors and textures can make a wall sizzle with excitement, particularly if they cover over years of dirt.

One of the things families most want to cover over are paint and crayon marks from their children. It's one thing to encourage that budding Picasso to finger-paint on butcher paper on the kitchen table. It's quite another to have your child turn the white walls of your home into a more permanent museum exhibition of avant-garde wall art. (I learned the hard way to never ask your child "What is this?" unless you want them to feel insulted. Instead, simply and slyly say, "Tell me about your painting.")

Thankfully our local hardware stores seem to have an endless supply of paint and all the tools needed to give my job that professional touch. Not that my walls ever look professionally painted, mind you, but I do my best.

Jesus had some rather harsh words for the religious leaders of his day. At one point, calling attention to their hypocrisy, he called them "whitewashed tombs full of dead men's bones" (Matthew 23:27). In other words, these supposed men of God looked like they were full of life. They had a fresh coat of paint over their lives, and because that's all people could see, they looked like they had it all together.

But in truth, they were using the whitewash to cover over the fact that they were like tombs. There was death in their hearts, not life. They had missed the message of freedom that Jesus had come to proclaim. Their lives were filled with judgment and scorn for others. There isn't enough paint in the world to cover up the mask of hypocrisy.

Fortunately, Jesus had another option. He would paint their sin-stained hearts with the red blood of his life, and somehow they would become as clean as newly fallen snow.

And truthfully, they should've seen it coming. It wasn't the first time God had covered over sin. Way back in the garden of Eden, when the man and the woman had sinned, they realized they needed to cover over their sin and their shame. Fig leaves were in abundant supply in the garden, so Adam and Eve fashioned crude clothes—the first ever—and hoped for the best.

But God sees through our feeble attempts to hide our sin. In our futile attempts to cover up, we tell lie after lie and try to make ourselves look better to others than we really are. We're no different than the Pharisees.

In his mercy, however, God didn't leave the man and the woman to cover their own sin. Instead, the life of an innocent beast in the garden was taken, and God provided a more suitable covering for the sin and shame of the couple. Blood had been spilled, and the man and the woman began to learn an important lesson that would be repeated throughout Scripture: "Without the shedding of blood there is no forgiveness" (Hebrews 9:22).

Notice, though, that Adam and Eve still bore the consequences of their sin. Giving birth to a child in labor would prove painful and difficult for the woman, and tilling the soil to give birth to a harvest of food would prove painful and difficult for the man. And the ultimate consequence was that they would die, and their bodies would return to dust.

There is a table in my dining room, one that my wife grew up with. Her father had taken scaffolding boards from an old project at work, and recycled them. He planed them so they would fit securely together, then clamped them up with dowels and glue. The table looks wonderful, but the table top itself has unique markings on it. Scars from red-hot rivets. Indentations where tools were dropped on the boards. An old nail hole.

The dark stain over the tabletop has brought out the beauty in the wood, but the scars from its past still remain. In the same way, God covers over our sin by forgiving us, but the consequences—the marks—of our sin still remain.

Apprenticeship: *Jesus, thank you for covering my sin. Paint my life with your mercy and charity and your spirit of forgiveness toward others. May the scars and wounds of my life serve as reminders of the pain and futility of sin, and thus keep me from willful wrongdoing. May I always be quick to acknowledge my sin, slow to hide it from you, and may I always submit to the brushstrokes of the Master Painter as he makes my life fit for heaven.*

GRAIN AND COLOR

The LORD said to Moses, "Speak to Aaron and his sons and to all the Israelites and say to them: 'If any of you—either an Israelite or an alien living in Israel—presents a gift for a burnt offering to the LORD, either to fulfill a vow or as a freewill offering, you must present a male without defect from the cattle, sheep or goats in order that it may be accepted on your behalf.'"

—Leviticus 22:17-19

Oak and walnut have a classic look to their color and grain, but they are rather common in furniture. Sometimes I want something a bit more exotic. I love the 3–D look of quilted maple, and zebrawood just plain looks cool. Bubinga is kinda funky, and the burl of any species can be a fun piece to turn. Tiger maple is a head-turner, and Australian Lacewood can look like one of those doilies your grandmother used to make.

I'm fascinated by the different species of trees and the grain and color they yield. When God created the heavens and the earth, He didn't skimp on the details. Consider the wood you work with for just a moment.

The history of a tree can be determined by looking at the rings on the stump and by the grain on the lumber it yields. Periods of drought and disease along with constant windy conditions can make for some interesting grains and figures in wood. Dormant buds that never branched out and developed cause burls, those rounded outgrowths that can look ugly on the outside but yield some great woodworking possibilities on the inside.

Obviously, the color saturation of a piece of wood gets our attention real quick. We all prefer working with heartwood, from the inner part of the tree, but sometimes you don't have a choice but to use a piece that also contains sapwood. Spalted wood is some of the most beautiful for turners, but because it is degraded wood that is literally rotten with a fungus, it isn't stable enough for construction purposes. But take a light piece of birch with those reddish spalted veins running through it, and you can turn a bowl that will be a conversation starter on any coffee table.

People have color, grain, and a certain amount of spalt, too. We all come from different backgrounds and cultures and races. God created us all with certain natural tendencies, but we all have different gifts and personalities. Just like an experienced woodworker can look at the grain of a piece of wood and tell something about the history of the tree, we can look at the personality traits and character of others and see a little of what God has brought them through in their lifetimes.

God in his wisdom has constructed a world where there are many different species of wood, featuring many unique grain patterns, and he has done the same with people. But while we enjoy the variety of wood grains and colors, why are we inclined to want people to be just like us?

Is that true in your life? Do you find yourself wanting to be around people who think just like you do, who enjoy the same things you do, and who believe the same way you do?

In the world God created, this isn't so easy. There are all those other "grains," those people who see life differently, who come from different backgrounds and cultures and races, who have different personalities and skill sets, people who even understand the God of the Bible a little differently.

According to the passage from Leviticus, God accepts the sacrifice, the worship, of "aliens," people who look and talk and act and think different from "us." We too often try to separate from those that are different. We let our politics, our worship styles, our skin colors, our personality grains rip us apart the way a crosscut blade separates wood. Ironic, isn't it? God, who has every reason to turn his back on us, still accepts anyone who comes to him in faith. But we, who have every reason to join together out of our need for strength in community, go through life splintering and breaking off, refusing to accept one another.

The colossal Sequoia trees of Northern California and Oregon are a national treasure. Many of them are taller than a football field is long, which means there's not enough line in your chalk box to mark one for ripping with your circular saw. Not that you'd want to anyway. These redwoods are too beautiful to harvest merely for their wood. Many have stood for a thousand years or more, through coastal storms and wind, as a silent picture of God's might and majesty. But the secret to their strength is not in what we see on top, but in what lies beneath the ground.

Ever wonder why you usually don't see one giant redwood tree growing by itself, miles from any others? It's because redwood trees actually have a very shallow root system. With its massive limbs acting like sails to catch the wind, a Sequoia would likely topple long before it reached its potential height of three hundred feet. But the redwoods interlock their roots with one another, providing a support system that helps sustain them through years of tempest and trial. They gain their strength by being part of a community, not by standing alone.

Vanilla ice cream is great, but boring if that's all you ever taste. A woodworker who only utilizes poplar is missing out on some great experiences working with cocobolo and tiger maple. And a church that refuses to recognize and accept the worship of others is simply in denial. Someday in heaven, we will be surrounded by the different grains and colors and patterns of people from every nation, tribe, people, and language. On that day, all splintering and branching off will cease. We will stand together in unity, just as God designed the Coastal Redwoods to hold hands underground, and we will sing the same song from Revelation 7:10, one we will all finally agree on: Salvation belongs to our God, who sits on the throne, and to the Lamb.

Apprenticeship: *Great God of creation and diversity, so much of my prejudice and pride is hidden from others, and I'm blind to much of it myself. Please forgive me for getting caught up in my own little world, as if everyone of any consequence is like me, and those who are unlike me are of little importance. At times I have been arrogant and tried to stand alone, and I have rejected others that you freely accept. I confess I need to hold hands with others and receive strength and encouragement and nourishment from them. Only then will I be able to withstand the storms of life.*

May I not wait until I get to heaven to enjoy unity with other believers. Help me to admire the beauty of the color and grain of others, and join with them now in worship of you, that we might begin to blessed by a little heaven on earth.

EVEN THE BACK SIDE

Woe to those who go to great depths to hide their plans from the LORD, who do their work in darkness and think, "Who sees us? Who will know?"

You turn things upside down, as if the potter were thought to be like the clay!

Shall what is formed say to him who formed it, "He did not make me"?

Can the pot say of the potter, "He knows nothing"? . . .

In that day the deaf will hear the words of the scroll, and out of gloom and darkness the eyes of the blind will see.

Once more the humble will rejoice in the LORD; the needy will rejoice in the Holy One of Israel.

—Isaiah 29:15-16, 18-19

I t is amazing to me that a tiny religious movement in America could so shape the landscape of woodworking and fine furniture. The Shakers were never very large in number—around six thousand at their peak in the 1800s—and certainly not all of them were woodworkers. But those who were brought a sense of spirituality and skill to each piece of furniture they built.

The Shaker style is one of my absolute favorites. Clean lines, precise layouts, no wasted space or unnecessary accoutrements. Everything utilitarian. Yet Shaker pieces also carry an elegant sensibility about them. But it's that marriage of their theology and their craft that fascinates me. Their simple service to God and others is a stark contrast to our materialistic world today. Materials and resources were closely managed. Nothing was created to call attention to itself; nothing was wasted on extravagance. Except . . .

Have you ever looked at the drawers on a vintage Shaker cabinet?

The drawers on a true antique Shaker cabinet (not a modern knock-off like I would make) are finished on the backside. The same number of coats of stain that were applied to the front of a drawer were also applied to the back. And at first glance, this doesn't seem to fit into Shaker thought and practice. Why would someone apparently waste a good resource, putting stain on the reverse side of a piece of furniture. Who would ever see it?

God.

In Shaker theology, they knew that God sees everything, including the back of the drawer, and that was enough for them. They wanted their work—all of their work—to reflect his excellence and be pleasing to him. This brings up an interesting question: Why do we live as if God doesn't see everything in our lives?

Scripture certainly bears out the fact of God's omniscience. The phrase "the eyes of the Lord" occurs eighty eight times in the Bible. Verses like Proverbs 15:3, "The eyes of the LORD are everywhere, keeping watch on the wicked and the good," and 2 Chronicles 16:9, "For the eyes of the Lord range throughout the earth to strengthen those whose hearts are fully committed to him," are great examples of God's all-seeing power. Most of the eighty-eight verses seem to show examples of people who either did evil or did good "in the eyes of the Lord." From the astronomic to the microscopic, God can see it all.

But perhaps the saddest example of the phrase is from the life of King Amaziah, who in 2 Chronicles 25:2, is described like this: "He did what was right in the eyes of the LORD, but not *wholeheartedly*" (italics mine). In other words, Amaziah wasn't the kind of guy who would put stain on the back of drawers to finish them. He had an appearance of godliness on the outside. But he wasn't fully committed to the Lord on the inside.

There's a real danger in assuming that God doesn't see everything, that we can hide sin in our hearts from God. And it's even worse to assume that if he does see our sin, he won't do anything about it. Isaiah says this is upside-down thinking, as if to say God is just like us—blind at times to sin. It's just crazy to believe that God doesn't see and understand what is going on in our lives.

Isaiah then gives us the solution to our dilemma in 29:18-19. When we begin to read the words of the scroll, God's Holy Word, then our eyes are opened. We begin to understand that God does see all and know all, that we can't hide our plans or our ways from him. We embrace a fresh humility and experience a vital joy in our walk with Christ.

Are there things you like to do in the dark? Places you like to go where you think no one will see you? Have you fallen for the delusion that God will simply wink at disobedience in your life? Are you making plans without consulting him?

Get into his book. Begin to humble yourself before him. That's the beginning of a life that serves God *wholeheartedly*.

Apprenticeship: *Omniscient, omnipotent, omnipresent God, I confess the craziness of my life before you. The thought that I could ever hide anything from you or "pull the wool over your eyes" is a form of temporary insanity, and I ask your forgiveness for living in darkness instead of in your glorious light. How could I ever believe you to be less than you are? I bring my condition to you, and ask you to give me the mind of Christ and fill my heart with the truth about who you are.*

FINISHING TIME

Listen to my cry for help, my King and my God, for to you
I pray.

In the morning, O LORD, you hear my voice; in the morning I lay my requests before you and wait in expectation.

—Psalm 5:2-3

I am still confident of this: I will see the goodness of the
LORD in the land of the living.

Wait for the LORD; be strong and take heart and wait for
the LORD.

—Psalm 27:13-14

The house we purchased in the spring of 2001 had a fireplace, but no mantel. Since it was our turn to host family and friends on Christmas Eve that
year, I decided late in the fall to build one. I figured, a little plywood here,

a little molding there, how hard can it be?

Building it out of pine, I knew that the piece could prove difficult when it came time to stain and finish. (Before the reader slays me for using pine, you should know that our home is rather country and informal, so a rich wood like walnut or mahogany would have looked out of place. Maybe in the next house . . . .) Stain tends to look blotchy on pine without a few coats of oil on it first. But if stain is applied after oiling the work, it can come out nice and even. So after the mantel was finished, I began hand-rubbing layer after layer of tung oil into the wood. After several layers I applied several layers of stain, each time getting the piece a little darker. Six layers of stain may seem much, but the pine took the stain much slower over the layers of oil. After that I put on a couple of coats of polyurethane, sanding between coats. Finally, I dressed it with some darkening wax that added a hint of patina to the mantel.

Of course, each layer I applied to the mantel required drying time. I built the mantel in a weekend, but the finish time took nearly two weeks longer! I got the piece attached above the fireplace a couple days before Christmas, just in time for the holidays.

Waiting on a finish to dry is never fun. They say a watched pot never boils. In today's vernacular, a watched website never loads. I can attest that polyurethane doesn't dry as you putter around the shop, checking it every thirty minutes with your finger! And the humidity of Houston doesn't speed up anything trying to dry.

Waiting on God is not fun, either. Too often we want to rush the process, get his work over and done in our lives so we can be put up on display, like the mantel. But what you are waiting for is not nearly as important as what God does in your life while you are waiting. He's developing the character you need for the next step, the next level, of your life.

The Bible still speaks to our needs today. In the middle of a culture hooked on instant messaging, the word "wait" occurs 135 in the Old and New Testaments. Surely that is no accident—it must be a concept that God wanted us to incorporate into our lives.

Waiting on God means to trust his timing for the events of our lives. It assumes that we worship a God who is in control of this universe, and that nothing can happen to us apart from his allowing it to happen. It is a faith that sustains us in difficult times, for even when we don't feel his presence, we know he is there and has not withdrawn his love from us.

To wait on God also means to reject the easy way out, to refuse to walk down the road that leads to a rejection of God and his ways. It is to hold fast to what God's Word says, and refuse to deviate from it.

We are promised that the very same God who began a good work in us will continue to work on our lives to completion (Philippians 1:6). Since I'm so far from completion, I'm assured that God will not be very far from me, for he has so much work to do in my life!

Are you waiting for the Lord? Are you keeping watch daily for any sign of activity from on high? "The Lord is not slow in keeping his promise, as some understand slowness," Peter reminds us in 2 Peter 3:9. He *will* come to you and speak to you and move on your behalf. Just take heart and wait.

Apprenticeship: *Lord, waiting is so hard, even painful. I don't deal with silence very well. It makes me uncomfortable when I don't hear you speak, and makes me feel that I need to do some talking and planning and scheming so the finish coats of my life will turn out right.*

But I know if I lean on my own understanding of life, I might well ruin the luster of your work (Proverbs 3:5-6). Remind me that you are doing a deeper work in me; refining the texture of my life, smoothing the raised spots on my surface, slowly creating something that will reflect your glory. You are hand-rubbing the finish deep into the pores of my heart, applying layer after layer of character that will bring out your beauty in my life. Develop your patience in me as I wait, I pray, and give me assurance that every time you polish me, I look a little more like my Savior.

CLEANING UP

> In a large house there are articles not only of gold and silver,
> but also of wood and clay; some are for noble purposes and
> some for ignoble. If a man cleanses himself from the latter,
> he will be an instrument for noble purposes, made holy, use-
> ful to the Master and prepared to do any good work.
>
> —2 Timothy 2:20-21

Why do we clean up after a project? It's not because of the phrase "Cleanliness is next to godliness." That sounds good, even spiritual, but it's not found anywhere in the Bible. God does expect us to be good stewards of that with which the Lord entrusts us, and that means taking care of our tools and workspaces. But you are not one iota more spiritual because you can eat off the floor of your shop. So, why do we clean up after a project?

For starters, it looks better. And a clean workspace is a much safer workspace. Too many accidents occur when tools and materials are lying around on the floor of the shop, or when your table saw doubles as a potting table for those perennials you've been meaning to plant.

We also clean our tools so they will last longer. We put things away so that we can get ready for the next project. And let's be truthful—we clean up out of respect for others, so we'll keep our spouses happy!

All of these are valid reasons, but it doesn't help me enjoy cleaning up any more. For me, sanding a project smooth is a day off at the beach compared to washing out paint brushes and sweeping up the garage floor. But it has to be done, and since I'm the one who made the mess....

Have you ever watched one of those organizational shows on TV? A professional expert surveys the battle zone of a typical American home where the husband and the wife have held on to too many physical memories of the past. The husband has a comic book collection, a surfboard he hasn't used in seventeen years, a run-down moped taking up space in the garage, and retro clothes that (hopefully) will never be in style again. The wife has a set of paints and canvases from when she went through her artist phase, an old guitar, a doll collection, and old clothes that she regrets she can't fit into anymore.

The expert comes in and recommends that they have a bonfire, or at least a garage sale. But under no circumstances, the expert warns, should the couple keep the stuff. They whine and fuss and pout, and some even try to sneak some of their stuff back into the house. But the watchful eye of the expert catches them, and they are reminded of their original goal—to clean and organize and update their house into something they would be proud of.

The point is, before the couple can move forward with updating or remodeling their home, they have to clean up the junk and get rid of it. And the cleanup really does help them move forward. It gives them a new confidence; it makes room for new things and helps them move on from the past.

Usually, once the couple sees the drastic makeover in their home, they wonder why they held onto their old stuff for so long.

Spiritual clutter accumulates over time. It doesn't just move into the home of our heart overnight. When we don't set aside regular time for confession of sin and cleansing, the junk piles up in our hearts. We become so attached to our spiritual baggage that we can't imagine living without it. We forget how it got there, but we assume there's no getting rid of it.

But when we allow the Lord to do a cleansing work in our lives, we allow him to prepare us for the next step, the next project, the next makeover. We become a useful space in God's hands, to be used for noble purposes. After all, isn't the workroom itself a "tool" in the worker's ability to craft?

In the context of Paul's letter to Timothy, Paul counsels his young apprentice on how to stay uncontaminated from false teachers and remain set apart for God's service. The apostle's admonition isn't just for young pastors, but it is for anyone who wants to follow Christ. A useful vessel is in a constant state of being cleaned up, of being made holy by God. And that is the biggest reason to clean up, that we might be tools that are useful to the Master.

Ready to move on with a spiritual remodeling project? Go back—once—and ask the Lord to clean you up. First John 1:9 is a daily bar of soap each Christ-follower should shower with. It says, "If we confess our sins, he is faithful and just and will forgive us our sins and purify us from all unrighteousness." Once you've confessed those sins, you never need revisit them again.

Apprenticeship: *Lord, no wonder I don't feel like you use me very often to accomplish your noble purposes. There's too much clutter in this workshop to get much done. I've let the place go, and it's gotten so filthy that as I look at the warehouse of my heart, I don't even know where to begin.*

It's going to be painful, too, I know. When you look me in the eyes and tell me I need to pitch some of the hatred and greediness and untruths in my life, I know it needs to be done. And I know I need to obey. So why do I find myself clinging to these worthless things that turn my clean workshop into a useless, unsafe factory where little of any value is produced?

Lord, remind me that you never ask me to give up something where you don't replace it with something much better. Forgive me for making an idol of these things in my life and for thinking there's more fulfillment in sin than in following you. Would you start the cleansing process in my heart? Today?

PRICING YOUR CREATION

God saw all that he had made, and it was very good. And there was evening, and there was morning—the sixth day.

—Genesis 1:31

Remember the Sabbath day by keeping it holy. Six days you shall labor and do all your work, but the seventh day is a Sabbath to the LORD your God.

—Exodus 20:8-10

My father-in-law used to load up a trailer full of things he had made, and haul his wares to a booth at craft shows. Often these would be various kinds of boxes, decorative items, and small pieces of furniture. Occasionally he would ask me if I had anything to display alongside his inventory. Sometimes I would give him some small boxes and clocks to sell for me, but I always struggled to know how much to ask for them. It's a tricky process, and it is very easy to overprice or undervalue your inventory. If you price items according to what you think you should make by the hour as a woodworker, it can be discouraging. Ultimately, I ended up looking around at the prices of similar items, and tried to appraise my merchandise accordingly, hoping somebody would walk down the aisle of the craft show, see my work, and decide on the spot, "I've gotta have it!"

But what do you do when there are no precedents, when you've got a particularly creative item that has never been seen before?

After each day of creation, God stepped back and assigned value to his work. "It is good," he said over and over in Genesis 1. And on day six, after he had created male and female, he said, "It is *very* good." And then God rested on the Sabbath.

Notice that God declared the worth of Adam and Eve before they had accomplished a single thing. Think of it—Adam hadn't been elected chairman of the board, pastored a megachurch, or won the Super Bowl. Eve hadn't completed award-winning medical research, or closed multi-million dollar deals or written a best-seller. They were just the first people created, with no precedent for their value. Nothing like them had ever been created before, and God declared them to be very good.

We would do well to learn how to declare our lives to be very good. And it all starts when we choose to "remember the Sabbath day by keeping it holy" (Exodus 20:8). In our age of speedy Internet connections, microwave ovens, and "instant" everything, a commandment that calls us to slow down seems antiquated. But when we take time for regular rest and worship, we can assess the right value to our work and our lives, because we remember to whom they are properly dedicated.

I could arbitrarily set a price on one of my clocks at $35. But is it really worth that? In truth, the price is set by whatever the highest bidder is willing to pay for my clock on the open market. That may be $35, but it may be only $15.

Does it surprise you that God likes to roam the midways and booths of craft shows? And he looks over the merchandise on the table until he sees you, and then decides he's got to have you. But a quick check of your price tag reveals an extreme price. The price tag on your life simply reads "The Cross."

And God says, "That's a high price indeed. But I'll gladly pay it."

What are you really worth? Sometimes we get locked into our work at the salt mine or the assembly line and can get discouraged, particularly if we feel we are not compensated very well. It's easy to equate our self-worth with the bottom line on our paychecks and the size of our office at work. We all want to be assured that our work is significant beyond how much we are paid, that our life and labor matter to someone.

But ultimately, you are worth whatever the highest bidder is willing to pay for your life. God has already paid that price. He did it at Calvary, laying down his life in such a way that makes multi-million dollar acquisitions look puny. He decided you were his "gotta have it" purchase, and he was willing to pay the price to acquire you.

Listen for God's voice today. He calls out to us in the midst of our hurry-scurry world, "You are good! I created you and take great delight in you! I've got to have you! Follow me and let me ascribe great worth to your life and your work."

Apprenticeship: *God of all creation, I did not create myself. You created me. Show me how I can see my life through your eyes and how I might benefit from consistent Sabbath rest. Slow me down, Lord. May I play at my worship no more, and may my work take on the significance that you desire it to have. Forgive me for making my work an idol. I surrender my career, my hobbies, and my income to you. May I worship only you today and every day.*

LEGACY

O my people, hear my teaching; listen to the words of my mouth. I will open my mouth in parables, I will utter hidden things, things from of old- what we have heard and known, what our fathers have told us.

We will not hide them from their children; we will tell the next generation the praiseworthy deeds of the LORD, his power, and the wonders he has done.

He decreed statutes for Jacob and established the law in Israel, which he commanded our forefathers to teach their children, so the next generation would know them, even the children yet to be born, and they in turn would tell their children.

Then they would put their trust in God and would not forget his deeds but would keep his commands.

—Psalm 78:1-7

What have you built that will outlast you? What will be cherished by your family when you're gone? Perhaps it's a cradle, to be used by succeeding generations of young mothers who will rest safe in the notion that their babies will sleep secure in a bed fashioned with love by an ancestor they never met. Maybe you hope a young mother will be comforted in the middle of the night as she runs a hand over the well-worn armrest of a rocking chair while she prays a colicky baby back to sleep. Or maybe it's a dining room table, and you envision a young family making memories around a meal, maybe even thanking God for his provision in their lives.

I'm not a man of great means, nor am I a master woodworker. I hope I have not passed myself off to the reader as something I am not. But among my worldly possessions there are some wooden boxes, pens, and crafts that I hope kindle some reminiscence in my children. There's a kitchen table and a couple of benches that should get some use in the coming years. And I have plans for future projects that should help provide for future generations.

At some point, each of us wrestles with the questions of legacy. "Have I made a difference? Will I leave this world better off than it was when I entered it? Have I done something that will last for eternity? Will I be remembered as someone who gave more than I took?"

If you have a family, the questions loom larger: "What have I left for my children, and their children? Beyond some sort of financial trust, what will they have learned from me that will enrich and better their lives and the lives of their families?"

King David learned too late in life that legacy is not something you begin working on near the end of your life. Instead, it is the sum total of your life. Though David had served as a great king and a "man after God's heart," the consequences of his sin were borne out in the lives of his children. He had reproduced his strengths in his children, but he had also passed down his weaknesses. As a crowning achievement of his own legacy, he longed to build a final temple to the Lord. But in what had to be a stunning blow to his ego and self-made plans, God told David that he would not be the one to build the temple. That honor would go to his son, Solomon.

But even though David would not be the builder, the Spirit of God had given him great plans for that magnificent house of worship, and all the buildings around it. David passed those plans down to his son (1 Chronicles 28:11-12) and also made financial provision for the building (1 Chronicles 29:2-5). David left a legacy. It was not as big as he might've wished, but he purposed at the end of his life to do what he could to touch the future.

There are at least four to six generations mentioned in the passage from Psalm 78: the fathers (v. 3), the present generation (v. 4), their children (v. 4), the children yet to be born (v. 6), and children of those yet to be born (v. 6). And just what is it that these men of old were encouraged to pass down? Some family heirloom? Some priceless piece of furniture or treasured work of art? They were challenged to pass down the Word of God, so the coming generations "would put their trust in God and would not forget his deeds but would keep his commands" (v. 7). They were planting the acorns for generations of shade trees under whose branches they knew they would never sit.

Perhaps a great legacy of faith was passed down to you, maybe you are the first follower of Christ in your family. Whatever the case, the call on your life is to serve as a fully devoted follower of Jesus, that you and he together might make something of your life that continues to influence future generations for the sake of the kingdom. So work hard and work well at your craft, for when you are gone someone will make a judgment about your life based on the work that survives you. Allow yourself to be shaped and sanded and stained by Jesus himself, so that future generations may make a right judgment about the joys of living and growing in the workshop of the Master Carpenter.

Apprenticeship: *Lord, I thank you for the journey of my life thus far, and for the pilgrimage you will continue to lead me on. May I always live as an apprentice under your loving watchful care, that my life may make a difference in this world for the sake of your kingdom. I pray now for the succeeding generations of my family, even children and grandchildren yet to be born, that they too may trust you and keep your commands always.*

RESTORATION

I consider that our present sufferings are not worth comparing with the glory that will be revealed in us. The creation waits in eager expectation for the sons of God to be revealed. For the creation was subjected to frustration, not by its own choice, but by the will of the one who subjected it, in hope that the creation itself will be liberated from its bondage to decay and brought into the glorious freedom of the children of God.

We know that the whole creation has been groaning as in the pains of childbirth right up to the present time. Not only so, but we ourselves, who have the first fruits of the Spirit, groan inwardly as we wait eagerly for our adoption as sons, the redemption of our bodies.

—Romans 8:18-23

Furniture restoration is a booming business. Like any industry, it has its experts and its charlatans. If you've ever watched *Antiques Roadshow* on TV, you know exactly what I mean. I once watched as a person brought in a beautiful antique William and Mary–styled highboy cabinet with trumpet legs, and an expert appraiser examined the cabinet with a fine-tooth comb. Finally, with the cameras rolling and the hopeful person waiting in anticipation, the appraiser stated that the cabinet was indeed genuine, but because an amateur had restored it, using less than quality materials and methods, the cabinet was not worth near as much as it might have been.

I'm no expert restorer, and the fact that I've had to restore some of my own creations might suggest that I'm a less than quality woodworker to begin with! But over time, even the best-made chairs and benches need maintenance as the wood expands and contracts during the seasons, loosening the joints.

I wonder if people ever brought broken furniture to Jesus and asked him to fix it for them. Did they realize they were in the presence of the one who could restore their hearts as well?

But Jesus doesn't stop at renewing our hearts. Our entire planet is in desperate need of restoration. It is not just us who have felt the consequences of sin. No, the earth itself bears just a hint of its original unblemished glory. All we have ever known in this day and age are polluted rivers, diseased forests, extinct animals, stagnant lakes, declining natural resources, and shifting fault lines. Paul says that even the creation itself is waiting in eager anticipation for its redemption.

But there is coming a day when the old earth will be remade into the new earth (Revelation 21:1). The late Keith Green used to sing a song called "I Can't Wait to Get to Heaven," and in the song he sang the lyric "In six days You created everything/but You've been working on Heaven 2,000 years." As great and grand as our planet is to this day, it pales in light of what it will look like someday when it is fully restored. No longer under the curse of sin, it will be resplendent in its original glory, and it will be a perfect reflection of its Creator.

And our bodies will be completely restored too. No more disease and death. We will have perfect physical bodies that don't have need of glasses and dentures and pacemakers and pills. Every cell in our bodies will have been permanently and irrevocably restored to that condition which God originally intended.

Relationships will be restored, too. That old selfish nature the human race has operated with for so long will be gone. We'll be completely filled with love for others, and they'll be filled with love for us. Some brothers and sisters in Christ whom we can't stand in this life will be found working and living alongside us in the next. I know, it sounds improbable, and even like something you might not want right now. But our hearts will be so restored, there will finally be peace in the world. The nations will lay down their swords (Isaiah 2:4) and even the wolf will live with the lamb (Isaiah 11:6).

Will there be woodworking in heaven? I'm inclined to say "Yes," since God is a creator, and he has built his creativity into us. In fact, one of the primary ways we glorify him is by creating, whether it be writing a song, painting a picture, or building something out of wood. And just imagine how beautiful the trees of the New Earth will be! Our work and creativity as woodworkers will just be beginning the moment we set foot in heaven.

But all of this will only be possible if you allow God to restore your heart. Have you done that?

Apprenticeship: *Lord, I find myself in great need of restoration. Over the years I've tried to inject the glue of my own self-righteousness into the cracks and crevices of my life, and I've tried to hold things together. But self-repair will never take away the stain of my sin. Please forgive me of my sins, and come into my life. Come restore me and give me a new heart and the promise of a new life in which to serve you.*

And Lord, if there is woodworking in heaven, would you save me a spot at your workbench? I would love to continue to be your apprentice there, to learn more from your examples to me. I want to someday create a gift for you that will express my thanks to you for all you have done for me. Until then, may the life I live on this earth be sufficient to praise you.

NOTES

PLANS

1. Martin Luther King Jr., *Where Do We Go from Here: Chaos or Community?* (New York: Harper & Row, 1967), 89.

TEKTON

1. Justin Martyr, *Dialogue with Trypho*, 88.

MADE WITH WONDER

1. http://en.thinkexist.com/quotation/guido_the_plumber_and_michelangelo_obtained_their/199466.html

COST ANALYSIS

1. Dietrich Bonhoeffer, *The Cost of Discipleship* (New York: Simon & Schuster, 1959), 44.
2. Ibid., 45.
3. Ibid., 89.

TOOLS

1. G. Weilacher, Thinkexist.com. http://en.thinkexist.com/quotation/one_only_needs_two_tools_in_life-wd-to_make/10827.html
2. Charles Kingsley, *The Works of Charles Kingsley* (Philadelphia: John D. Morris & Company, 1899), 128.

RIGHT TOOL, RIGHT JOB

1. Abraham Maslow, Thinkexist.com. http://en.thinkexist.com/quotation/if_the_only_tool_you_have_is_a_hammer-you_tend_to/221060.html

THE TOOL YOU CAN'T LIVE WITHOUT

1. "Be Thou My Vision," traditional Irish hymn (trans. Mary E. Byrne).

MATERIALS

1. Antoine de Saint-Exupéry, Thinkexist.com. http://en.thinkexist.com/quotation/if_you_want_to_build_a_ship-dont_drum_up_people/170927.html
2. Dave Barry, *The Taming of the Screw* (Emmaus, PA: Rodale Press, 1983), 11.

FINISHING

1. Henry Ward Beecher, *Life Thoughts: Gathered from the Extemporaneous Discourses of Henry Ward Beecher* (Boston: Phillips, Samson & Company, 1858), 162.
2. Winston Churchill, Thinkexist.com. http://en.thinkexist.com/quotation/we_shall_neither_fail_nor_falter-we_shall_not/150162.html

SCRIPTURE INDEX

SCRIPTURE INDEX